WHO KNEW?

QUESTIONS

THAT WILL MAKE
YOU THINK AGAIN

Sarah Herman

The
History
Press

First published 2017

The History Press
The Mill, Brimscombe Port
Stroud, Gloucestershire, GL5 2QG
www.thehistorypress.co.uk

British Library Cataloguing in Publication Data.
A catalogue record for this book is available from
the British Library.

ISBN 978 0 7509 8446 1

Conceived, designed and produced by
QUID Publishing Ltd
Part of the Quarto Group
1st Floor Ovest House,
58 West Street,
Brighton BN1 2RA
www.quidpublishing.com

Design by Clare Barber
Text by Sarah Herman

Printed in China

'For Ian, for always keeping me guessing!'

CONTENTS

INTRODUCTION

There's nothing quite like being the biggest brainiac in the boardroom, the dinner party guest who really shows their knowledge, the office buddy who chimes in to settle an argument or the parent who passes wisdom on to their subjects (sorry, children).

Having the facts at your fingertips is one thing, but being able to explain who, what, where and why puts you a step above those quick-fire quizmasters. This book is all about expanding your mind and fuelling you with the answers to curious questions, many of which you might never have thought to ask. And all of which will leave you exclaiming, 'Who knew?'

Over the following chapters you'll get to grips with wild weather, bodily functions, outstanding artworks and mind-boggling botanicals. You'll travel back in time to the lands of the ancients, read up on the lives of authors and don your protective goggles for some good old-fashioned science. And if all that's not enough, take a trip around the world, get clued up on the origins of sports (whiff-whaff, anyone?) and arrive at the outer reaches of the galaxy.

From the silly ('Is it safe to eat watermelon snow?') and the scientific ('Is the periodic table complete?') to the unusual ('What happened to the Soviet space dogs?') and the unexpected ('What did Vladimir Nabokov keep in his cabinet?'), you'll soon be an expert on the brilliant and bizarre spectrum that *Who Knew?* covers. You'll be the one exhibiting your latest learnings by the water cooler and wowing your loved ones with tidbits of tantalising trivia.

Of course, all this reading is no good without retention. That's why, at the end of each section, there's a quick quiz to keep you on your toes. Test yourself and your friends with these pithy pickings from each chapter to make sure you know more than they do. You'll soon realise that while money and accolades are nice, knowledge (and being a smug smarty-pants) really is its own reward.

So get ready to galvanise your grey matter and sharpen your *savoir faire* as you step into the wondrous world of knowing it all – or, at the very least, knowing a lot more than you did before.

HAS IT EVER RAINED CATS AND DOGS?

WHAT'S THE HEAVIEST THING A TORNADO CAN CARRY?

WHAT IS A STORM BABY?

WHAT MAKES A SNOWSTORM A BLIZZARD?

IS IT SAFE TO EAT WATERMELON SNOW?

WEATHER AND CLIMATE

What's the difference between fog and mist?

Fog and mist are pretty much the same thing – a type of dense, low-lying stratus cloud, made up of droplets of water. The extent to which they obscure visibility is what determines which word is appropriate.

How Far Can You See?

The term 'fog' is used when visibility to the naked eye is less than 180 metres. However, in the context of shipping and aviation, 1,000 metres is the internationally recognised distance, so anything where visibility is greater than this is considered mist.

Haven't the Foggiest

While fog and mist can be beautiful and enchanting, adding a sense of mystery to landscapes and mountaintops, these tricky weather types have caused a few problems in their time. In 1815, panic swept Great Britain after a message announcing Wellington's victory at Waterloo, relayed by semaphore line from the English coast to London, was obscured by heavy fog. Instead of communicating 'Wellington defeated Napoleon at Waterloo,' the message read 'Wellington defeated.'

HISTORY'S DEADLIEST FOG

Until the Clean Air Acts of 1956 and 1968, London was well known for its heavy smog, created from pollutant chimney smoke mixing with the city's damp air. Known as 'pea-soupers' because of their thick nature and sulphurous fumes, these smogs were reported as reducing visibility to just 60 centimetres. In December 1952, an unlucky combination of weather conditions and factory fumes created the Great Smog, which lasted nearly five days, killing around 4,000 and causing health problems for many more.

Can lightning strike twice?

Lightning can travel at a speed of 22,500 kilometres per hour and a distance of 100 kilometres. While your chances of being struck are about one in three million, that doesn't mean that lightning hasn't struck the same person or location twice.

Unwanted Records

Park ranger Roy Cleveland Sullivan from Virginia, United States, was struck by lightning seven times between 1942 and 1977, making him the Guinness World Record holder for surviving the most lightning strikes. And the Empire State Building was once hit 15 times in one 15-minute storm.

HOTTER THAN THE SUN

When lightning strikes the ground, the energy heats the surrounding air to anywhere from 10,000 to 33,000°C – potentially six times hotter than the 5,500°C surface of the sun. Injuries sustained by people unlucky enough to be struck include temporary deafness, third-degree burns, and even cardiac arrest – but there's only a 10% chance of being killed.

The Lightning Chaser

American Founding Father and inventor Benjamin Franklin was among the first to hypothesise that metal conducts lightning. In 1752 he set out to prove the theory that lightning is a form of electricity. Although there is some scientific debate about how or even if the experiment was performed, it's thought that he tied a metal key to a kite with an insulating silk ribbon. When he flew the kite in a storm, the key was struck by lightning and the electric charge was captured in an early type of capacitor, called a Leyden jar, proving the theory. Fortunately, Franklin survived to tell the tale.

How fast can a sand dune move?

From Marco Polo and Alexander the Great to Genghis Khan, some of the world's most famous adventurers, conquerors and explorers have travelled across deserts to change the course of history. But you might not know that the sand dunes are travelling, too, at the mercy of the winds.

Carried Away

Sand dunes are formed when there's an abundance of sand with little vegetation to anchor it, a strong wind, and shrubs or rocks that obstruct the sand so it piles up. There are three ways that sand moves: suspension, creeping and saltation. Suspension – when a sand grain is blown high into the air by a very strong wind – only accounts for about 1% of sand dunes' movement. And creeping – when a grain bumps into another grain, causing them to jump or roll along – accounts for about 4%.

Bouncing Along

Saltation is when the wind lifts the grains a few inches above the ground and drops them a couple of inches away, causing them to bounce and be lifted again. This is predominantly how sand moves.

As the sand builds up on the windward side of a dune, gravity takes hold and the grains at the top eventually fall over the other side, either as a trickle or in small avalanches. Eventually the whole face of the dune will collapse.

The Sands of Time

How quickly the dune moves depends on the wind speed, the dune's size and the amount of vegetation in its path: the more vegetation there is, the more the dune will be obstructed, slowing it down. Smaller dunes – those less than 6 metres high – are formed from less sand, so they move much more quickly and can travel as much as 12 metres per year. Some dunes in Great Sand Dune National Park in Colorado, United States, where wind speeds reach 65 kilometres per hour, have been known to move around 1 metre per week. Barchan dunes – identified by their crescent moon shape – measure 9 to 30 metres high and over 370 metres wide, and typically move up to 4 metres per year. They're commonly found in open inland regions, including Turkestan and the Namib Desert.

DEVOURED BY THE DESERT

Those living in or near the desert, or beside a sandy coastline, have a constant battle to stop their home from being consumed by the stuff. Some towns have been swallowed whole. On the banks of the Kalamazoo River, near the mouth of Lake Michigan, in the United States, are some large sand dunes – the only marker of a once-booming waterfront town called Singapore. In the mid-1800s, Singapore was a port city and shipbuilding behemoth, profiting from the abundant wood in the surrounding forests. After the Great Chicago Fire of 1871, the demand for timber rose to unprecedented levels. As a result, Singapore's loggers caused mass deforestation to the area. Without the protective tree cover, the city was left exposed to the constant wind, and the sand was free to move without obstruction. Within four years, Singapore had disappeared under the dunes forever.

What's the heaviest thing a tornado can carry?

The United States experiences on average 1,000 tornadoes each year, a large percentage occurring in Tornado Alley in the south-central states. Tornadoes can be extremely powerful, causing tremendous damage, but due to their unpredictability and often remote locations, many go undocumented. When they are spotted, they can be hard to measure.

How Do Tornadoes Form?

Tornadoes are the result of a convective 'supercell' thunderstorm – an organised storm that contains a strong, rotating updraft. Tornadoes form inside the storm when warm, moist air on the ground converges with cool, dryer air farther up that's moving in the opposite direction. This is known as wind shear and produces a spinning tube of air. This speeds up inside the storm, creating a funnel cloud, which then descends to earth in a vertical tube. With the right conditions, tornadoes can pick up so much air, dirt, and debris that they can grow to over a kilometre wide. The fastest tornadoes can move at speeds of more than 100 kilometres per hour, with wind speeds inside a tornado believed to be up to 512 kilometres per hour.

Heavy Lifters

In *The Wizard of Oz*, a fictional tornado whisked up Dorothy's farmhouse and all its contents; in real life, the larger items that tornadoes can carry tend to be vehicles. Updraft suction and vertical velocity near the tornado's core help to pick up these large objects, and it's not unusual for them to carry vans weighing more than 1 metric ton.

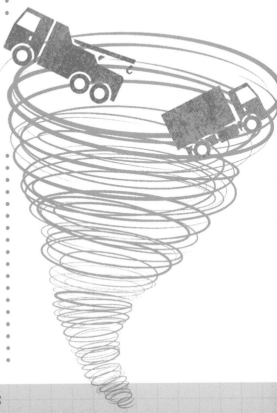

However, in 1990 a tornado in southwestern Texas, United States, was feeling greedy and managed to move three oil tanks around 5 kilometres east of their production facility. They are estimated to have weighed a combined 80 metric tons. This is believed to be the heaviest thing a tornado has carried.

FAR, FAR AWAY

Small objects get swept up into tornadoes all the time. While they might not be as impressive in stature as a car or a truck, they can travel a lot farther. In 1995, University of Oklahoma researchers started studying the pattern of debris deposited by tornadoes. Over five years they were sent more than 1,000 objects whose origin location could be identified, such as a bowling jacket with the owner's name stencilled on the back. Most of the objects had travelled 25 to 30 kilometres, but the farthest was 240 kilometres.

Twister Turmoil

Fortunately, most tornadoes do not result in death. Advanced weather warning systems mean communities are often given sufficient notice to move out of a tornado's path or take shelter. The largest number of fatalities from a single tornado occurred in the United States in 1925, when 695 people from Missouri, Indiana and Illinois died, while 2,027 were injured. In more recent years, in 2011, one of the deadliest tornadoes struck the city of Joplin, Missouri, killing 158 and injuring over 1,000. The terrifying twister reached wind speeds of 322 kilometres per hour.

Is it safe to eat watermelon snow?

We all know to steer clear of yellow snow, but what about the pink stuff? In high-altitude and Arctic spots, where the snow never fully melts, the summer sun causes patches of it to turn the colour of a tantalising snow cone. But that's not tropical fruit syrup – it's algae!

Keeping Cool

Just like other wet surfaces the world over, snow provides a breeding ground for over 60 species of algae. The most common of these is *Chlamydomonas nivalis*, found in melting snowdrifts. This alga is not coloured pink, but to protect itself from UV rays it produces its own form of sunscreen that's full of carotenoids – brightly coloured UV-absorbing pigments – and it's these that make the alga red and the snow pink.

In late spring and summer, pinkish tones colour the landscape of sunny, snow-covered areas with low rainfall, and at depths of up to 25 centimetres if you start digging. These algal blooms spread quickly. The darker the colour of the snow, the less light it reflects. As the amount of light the snow reflects (known as albedo) decreases, it begins to melt more quickly. As the snow melts, more of its surface area becomes prime for the algae to breed, in turn changing the snow's colour and causing it to melt further.

IRONING OUT THE FACTS

While you'd be forgiven for thinking a large pinky patch of snow was the result of an expeditionary massacre, our forefathers had a different explanation. In 1818, when Captain John Ross sailed from England to chart Arctic waters, he came across large amounts of watermelon snow in Baffin Bay. In the absence of a freezer, the melted snow, which the *Times* reported resembled red port wine, was brought back to England for chemical testing, and was declared to be the result of meteoric iron deposits in the underlying rock.

Eat at Your Peril

Watermelon-tinted snow sounds like the perfect treat after a long hike in the sunshine, and a long hike is probably what you'll have to do to find any. As most pink snow is found at high latitudes or altitudes – think the Arctic, Antarctica and the Himalayas – you'll have to endure freezing temperatures and a long walk to find it. And even then, you might want to think twice – while it's technically safe to eat, scientists warn people against it due to the snow's laxative effect. Just think how far you'll be from a lavatory.

Going Green

Pink isn't the only unusual snow colour. Different algae have been known to cause chemical reactions that colour the snow orange and even green. The latter, known as *Chloromonas brevispina*, can be found in less sunny alpine areas, usually near tree canopies.

Has it ever really rained cats and dogs?

The English animal idiom to describe heavy rain is thought to have been in use long before it appeared in Henry Vaughan's *Olor Iscanus* (1651), and other languages have similar expressions. Absurd though it may seem, there are a number of recorded instances of animals actually raining from the sky, albeit not cats or dogs.

Weird Waterspouts

Waterspouts are the weather phenomenon responsible for animals falling from the sky. A waterspout is a whirling column of air and water mist, and there are two types – fair-weather and tornadic. While fair-weather waterspouts develop on the surface of large bodies of water and don't tend to travel, tornadic waterspouts are associated with severe thunderstorms. They form over the water, but sometimes these tornadoes can move towards land. Just like a land-based tornado, a waterspout might be strong enough to pick up animals living near the surface of the water, such as fish. If it then travels over land, the fish might find themselves deposited there.

Falling Fish, Frogs and Snails

While there is no hard evidence of animals travelling in a waterspout around the world, there are numerous reports of fish, frogs and snails falling from the sky. A rain shower of toads is recorded as far back as 1683 in the British county of Norfolk. In 1835 a shower of molluscs called *Bulinus truncates* fell on Montpellier, France, and in 1809 Lieutenant John Harriott wrote of some fishy weather occurring

Pondicherry, India, saying: 'a quantity of small fish fell with the rain, to the astonishment of all. Many of them lodged on the men's hats … but how they ascended or where they existed I do not pretend to account. I merely relate the simple fact.'

More recently, in Japan in 2009, a number of cities reported seeing tadpoles rain down from the sky. While there are suggestions that some frog 'showers' might just be a large jumping migration, waterspouts are believed to be responsible for at least some of these bizarre occurrences.

'There are numerous reports of fish, frogs and snails falling from the sky.'

AIRBORNE ALLIGATOR

A waterspout was the explanation given for an alligator found in 1843, on the streets of Charleston, South Carolina, in the United States. A report in the *Times-Picayune* described the alligator as being 60 centimetres long. It said: 'We have not been lucky enough to find anyone who saw him come down – but the important fact that he was there is incontestable – and as he couldn't have got there any other way, it was decided unanimously that he rained down. Besides, the beast had a look of wonder and bewilderment about him, that showed plainly enough he must have gone through a remarkable experience.'

What makes a snowstorm a blizzard?

Not all snowstorms can be classified as a blizzard. In order to earn the moniker, a snowstorm must meet three criteria: wind speed must be 30 knots (56 kilometres per hour) or more, visibility must be significantly reduced and the storm must last for at least three hours.

Bring on the Blizzard

If these three conditions aren't met, then the storm is normally classified as a 'winter storm' or 'heavy snow'. Although freezing temperatures often accompany blizzards, they're no longer a requirement for a storm to be considered one. In the past, blizzards were categorised by their temperature as well, with −30°C or lower being the benchmark. Other languages have different words to describe severe snowstorms. In Russian, there are four: *metel'* is used to describe wind-driven snow, *v'yuga* is a literary term for a snowstorm, and *buran* and *purga* describe region-specific blizzards.

SIBERIAN SNOWSTORMS

Russia has some of the world's fiercest snowstorms. The dreaded *purga* normally arrives in northern Siberia every winter. The storm travels from the north or northeast of the region and stampedes across the Kamchatka Peninsula. It's so strong and the air is filled with so much snow that people cannot open their eyes and struggle to breathe and stand upright. The extreme weather is disorienting to the point where people have been found frozen to death a short distance from their homes. The *buran* in southern Siberia is a different beast. While the temperatures are actually warmer, the snow-filled wind is so strong that it feels much colder. The Soviets named their first reusable spacecraft *Buran* after this impressive and powerful storm.

Chilling History

Some of the worst blizzards on record have taken place in the United States. More than 400 people died during the Great Blizzard of 1888, when up to 1.3 metres of snow were dumped on Massachusetts, Connecticut, New Jersey and New York. The coastal blizzard saw some 200 ships lost to the waves as well. The Super Bowl Blizzard of 1975 had a much lower human death toll of 58, but the heavy snowstorms in the Midwest took the lives of 100,000 farm animals that year. In more recent years, a 1993 blizzard received the title of 'Storm of the Century' because of the dramatic impact felt across the northeast of the United States and the loss of 300 lives. This region's blizzards are known as nor'easters.

DEADLIEST BLIZZARD

Due to dangerous driving conditions and freezing temperatures, blizzards pose a significant threat to human lives and are almost always deadly when they hit. The deadliest blizzard on record took place in Iran in 1972 and lasted for six days. Some villages were completely buried by the snow, and by the end of the ordeal an estimated 4,000 people had been killed.

Why does rain smell so good?

There's nothing quite like the smell after it's rained – perfumes and air fresheners have tried to capture it, but there's no substitute for the real thing. That smell has a name, 'petrichor', coined by two Australian scientists who in 1964 set out to determine the cause.

Smells Like Rain

The scientists figured out that a main cause is a blend of oils secreted by some plants when the earth is dry. When it rains, these oils are released into the air and mix with other substances, producing that unmistakable aroma. One of these, called geosmin, is made by bacteria in the soil. When the rain lands on the ground, it forces bacteria spores into the air with the geosmin, creating that wondrous whiff.

Anthropologically Speaking...

The fact that rain smells so good to humans could also be a result of evolution. Some studies have shown that the human nose can identify even highly diluted geosmin. Scientists studying Australia's Pitjantjatjara people observed a clear association between the smell of rain and the colour green. This sensory alliance illustrates a deep-rooted association in this often arid area between the season's first rain and the plant growth that usually follows it.

THUNDEROUS RECEPTION

There is sometimes a distinctive 'chlorine' smell in the air before a thunderstorm, the result of lightning splitting oxygen and nitrogen molecules in the atmosphere. They then reform as nitric oxide, which collides with other chemicals in the air to produce ozone. Ozone travels long distances, so you might indeed smell the storm coming.

Can two snowflakes be identical?

When Wilson Bentley started photographing snowflakes in 1885 in Jericho, Vermont, United States, the idea that no two snowflakes are alike was born. His photographs showed how, seen under a microscope, each snowflake's individual pattern was different. But that was over a century ago – surely someone's found a matching pair by now?

More Than Meets the Eye

Snowflakes, or snow crystals as they are more accurately called, are created when cloud-based water vapour cools and, rather than becoming liquid, it crystallises around microscopic dust particles. These crystals all start as small hexagonal plates, and the six 'arms' are formed where more water molecules land. As the crystal falls to earth, the humidity and temperature changes it encounters will inform its unique shape.

Look a Little Closer

It's possible (but unlikely) that two snowflakes could experience the same conditions in nature, causing them to appear identical. However, on a molecular level they can never match completely. Water molecules are made up of two hydrogen atoms and an oxygen atom, but not all hydrogen atoms are the same. While most consist of a proton and an electron, a few hundred out of every million also contain a neutron. This hydrogen isotope is called deuterium. Millions of water molecules make up a snowflake and one in three thousand of these contain deuterium instead of hydrogen. The vast number of variable positions of these molecules within the snowflake's structure means no two snowflakes can be completely identical.

Why are there no typhoons in the Atlantic?

A typhoon is a tropical storm with winds of 120 kilometres per hour. You won't find typhoons in the Atlantic, because when a tropical storm reaches that wind speed there, it's called a hurricane. The word 'typhoon' refers to extreme tropical storms in the western North Pacific.

The Eye of the Storm

Typhoons and hurricanes are both severe tropical cyclones – the generic term for a rotating storm system that starts out at sea. At the centre of any cyclone is the eye – the area around which the storm rotates. This can be anywhere between 20 and 50 kilometres in diameter. Underneath the eye, the sky above is often clear and the winds are less strong – it's usually the calmest point, the result of the strong winds converging around the eye wall but never reaching the eye itself.

It Came from the Sea...

The year 1780 was a particularly bad one for hurricanes in the Caribbean, but none were more catastrophic than the Great Hurricane of 10 and 11 October, one of the deadliest tropical storms of all time. It claimed the lives of an estimated 22,000 people, not to

mention the thousands who died as a result of the famine left in its wake. There was little to alert people to an impending hurricane, so Barbados's residents would have had no warning when the storm struck – flattening houses, capsizing ships and destroying sugar cane fields. Barbados wasn't the only island to face the storm's wrath – most of the eastern Caribbean was left in ruins.

What's in a Name?

While working in Australia, the 19th-century British meteorologist Clement Wragge devised a system using Greek letters and then mythological character names to keep track of local storms. When those ran out, Wragge named the worst storms after politicians to whom he'd taken a disliking.

During World War II, US meteorologists began naming Pacific storms after their wives and girlfriends. In the 1950s, a two-year period saw US storms officially named using the phonetic alphabet, a system abandoned in favour of women's names in 1953. This stuck, despite feminist protests, until 1978 for eastern North Pacific storms and 1979 for Atlantic storms, when men's names were added to the rotating roster. Now six lists of 26 names (one for each letter of the alphabet) are recycled every six years. Names are usually retired and replaced if a storm causes significant damage or loss of life.

STORM BABIES

A study published in 2010 in the *Journal of Population Economics* studied fertility data in relation to tropical storms affecting the Atlantic and Gulf Coast of the United States, to determine any correlation between people hunkering down for a storm and the number of babies that resulted. It found that when a 'watch' was issued, meaning a tropical storm could hit within 36 hours, there was a 2% surge in births nine months later. But when a more imminent 'warning' was issued, giving 24 hours' notice, the opposite effect occurred – up to a 2% decrease.

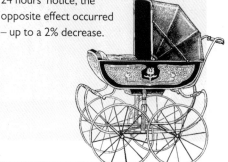

What do the Swiss have against snowmen?

The Swiss are a notoriously peaceful people – but not on the third Monday in April every year. That's the day crowds gather to see a snowman made from cotton paraded through Zurich. But don't be fooled by this charming pageantry – that snowman's life soon comes to a rather explosive end.

The End of Winter

Dating back to the 19th century, to mark the end of winter the Swiss celebrate Sechseläuten, which translates to 'ringing of the six o'clock bell'. Part of the festivities involves the parade of this 3-metre-tall fabric Frosty, known as a Böögg, which is stuffed full with dynamite. After making his way through town, he's placed on a bonfire. When the bells of Zurich's Grossmünster cathedral chime six o'clock in the evening, the bonfire is lit and soon after the snowman explodes. It's thought that the longer it takes for the Böögg to blow up, the longer it will be till spring arrives. The festival has taken place in this form annually since 1904, except for the World War II years when all green spaces were used to plant potatoes and there was nowhere to have the bonfire.

ARTISTIC SNOWMEN

Snowmen have been around since at least the Middle Ages and were often created by famous artists for the nobility. When Michelangelo was only 19, he was commissioned by the ruler of Florence to make one for his mansion's courtyard.

WEATHER AND CLIMATE

Test how much you've learned about the world's weird weather with this quick quiz.

Questions

1. 'Identical twin' snowflakes are identical on a molecular level – true or false?

2. How is the Swiss exploding Böögg snowman similar to Groundhog Day in North America?

3. What turns snow pink, and is it edible?

4. Which type of stratus cloud obscures visibility more – fog or mist?

5. Name one other word for blizzard.

6. Petrichor is a distinctive smell created by a blend of oils that are released when it rains – true or false?

7. Do sand dunes move faster or slower if there is lots of vegetation in their path?

8. Name at least one thing that waterspouts have dropped from the sky.

9. Benjamin Franklin experimented with lightning to prove it was a form of magic – true or false?

10. Typhoons occur in the Pacific, but what do they call extreme tropical cyclones that happen in the Atlantic?

Turn to page 244 for the answers.

WHAT DOES YOUR EYE COLOUR SAY ABOUT YOU?

HOW LONG AGO DID COSMETIC SURGERY BEGIN?

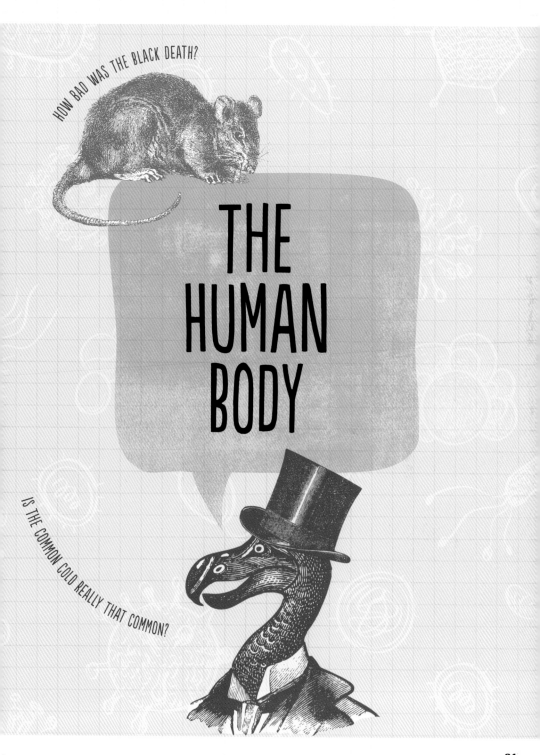

HOW BAD WAS THE BLACK DEATH?

THE HUMAN BODY

IS THE COMMON COLD REALLY THAT COMMON?

How bad was the Black Death?

The Black Death is regarded as one of the worst outbreaks of disease in history, killing some 75 million to 200 million people during the 1300s, including between 30% and 60% of Europe's population. The world's total population was so badly hit that it didn't recover for nearly 300 years.

Where Did It Come From?

The origins of bubonic plague are uncertain, although it is believed to have started in the Far East in the 1330s. Spread by germ-bearing fleas and carried by rodents, the disease made its way westward through trade routes, decimating populations in its wake. In the Byzantine Empire, they called it the Great Dying. It travelled north and west until it reached England by 1348, Norway in 1349 and finally northwest Russia in 1351.

Swift and Deadly

The initial symptoms were a fever and black, pus-filled boils (inflamed lymph nodes infected by the disease). Most of the infected died within two days. There was little in the way of relief, and no cure. While bubonic plague was caused by the bite of an infected flea, a less common version, called pneumonic plague (which developed when the infection spread to the lungs) could also be transmitted from an infected person via airborne droplets. Pneumonic plague had a mortality rate of 90–95%, compared to 30–75% for bubonic plague.

Can It Happen Again?

The black death eventually subsided, but it remains within animal populations and outbreaks occur from time to time. One of the things that limits the spread of plague is better personal hygiene, which was almost non-existent in the 1300s. Other factors that caused the original outbreak to diminish were bodies being burned instead of buried in mass graves, and people boiling drinking water. Of course, it is now known that the most effective measure is quarantine, which restricts outbreaks to small areas.

TRADING PLACES

While he can't really be blamed for the Black Death, Genghis Khan's insatiable conquest of the Far East had resulted in a Mongolian empire that stretched the length of the Silk Road. This meant that soldiers, traders and travellers were able to move freely along its length, quickening the speed at which the disease could spread to Europe. In China alone, 13 million people are believed to have died from it.

'The origins of bubonic plague are uncertain, although it is believed to have started in the Far East in the 1330s.'

Do blondes have more fun?

The familiar tropes about gentlemen preferring blondes and blondes having more fun were central themes in the films and advertising campaigns of the 1950s, and they endure to this day. But there is some scientific truth in the fact that blonde women are treated differently compared with brunettes and redheads.

'Blonde waitresses get more tips, and blonde hitchhikers are more likely to get picked up.'

DNA Doesn't Lie

While many people assume that hair colour is determined in large part by our DNA, and can even influence intelligence and personality, a study at Stanford University, United States, proved that it is in fact a single 'letter' out of 3.2 billion in our DNA code that signifies the difference between being blonde and another hair colour. The researchers turned up this 'blonde switch' in mice and could dramatically change their fur colour without changing the biology of any other part of the body.

Blondes Have More Funds

That's not to say there aren't societal and cultural differences to how blondes are perceived and treated. A study by the Queensland University of Technology, Australia, found that blonde Caucasian women earned over 7% more than their non-blonde peers. And it's not the only study to highlight the fact that blondes are financially rewarded for their hair colour. With that amount of extra cash, they can certainly afford to have more fun.

Gentlemen Approach Blondes

Several studies have pointed to the positive effects of being blonde – blonde door-to-door fundraisers receive more donations, blonde waitresses get more tips and blonde hitchhikers are more likely to get picked up. The effect that being blonde has on a woman's chances of being approached by men has also been widely researched. One study, which had a female subject wear different-coloured wigs in a nightclub over 16 nights, saw 127 men approach her when wearing a blonde wig, versus 84 for a brunette wig, 82 for a black wig and 29 for a redhead wig. So, while blondes might have the chance for more fun with men, they also have to fend off more unwanted advances.

Darwin's Blonde Moment

Victorian naturalist Charles Darwin wrote *On the Origin of Species*, which led to the theory of evolution by natural selection. A decade after that book's publication, he became interested in how hair colour might affect a woman's chances of marrying and reproducing, treating the question of whether blondes do have more fun quite seriously. Together with his son,

he studied data gathered by a doctor to ascertain whether English blondes were more likely to stay single, resulting in a decrease in blonde hair in the population. He made notes on the matter, but later decided the evidence was insufficient and that the higher rate of married brunettes was probably due to the natural darkening of hair with age.

What does your eye colour say about you?

They say the eyes are the window to the soul, and while it's a bit of a stretch to read minds by staring at someone intently, there are some revealing things to be learned from looking someone in the eye, including their ancestry, health, pain threshold and alcohol tolerance.

In Your Genes

Scientists used to think that one gene determined eye colour. They now know that there are multiple genes, as many as 13, that determine your eye colour. Two genes in particular – known as OCA2 and HERC2 – are responsible for eye colour, and you get one copy of each from each parent. These, combined with other colour-affecting genes, result in a veritable rainbow of possibilities. The genes determine how much of the pigment melanin is produced by the melanocyte stroma cells in your iris. The more melanin that's produced, the more brown your eyes will be. Scientists believe that up until about 6,000 to 10,000 years ago, all humans would have had brown eyes, but a genetic mutation created a switch, preventing the production of melanin and causing the first blue-eyed humans. Potentially, all blue-eyed people are descendants of a common ancestor.

Baby Blues

When babies are born, they have less melanin in their eyes, so the colour is often blue, and then by the age of three their true eye colour is known. While some babies of African or Asian descent are born with blue eyes, most are born with brown eyes due to the higher level of melanin in their eyes at birth. The biggest variety of eye colour can be seen in European populations, where brown is the most common, followed by blue or grey. Green is the rarest.

Health Alert

Eye colour has been researched in relation to specific health conditions, including vitiligo. American researchers who studied a sample of 3,000 sufferers of the skin condition found that it was significantly less common in blue-eyed people with European ancestry compared to those with tan or brown eyes. Lighter-colour eyes are more sensitive to UV rays, and are therefore at increased risk of melanoma of the uvea.

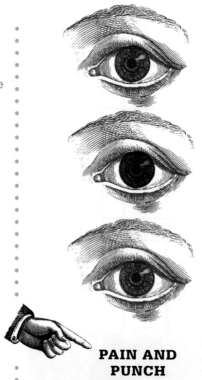

PAIN AND PUNCH

A study that investigated how women with different-coloured eyes experienced pain during childbirth indicated that those with darker-coloured eyes felt more physical pain and had more anxiety and depressive thoughts. On the positive side for those women, another study showed that their lighter-eyed counterparts could handle larger quantities of alcohol and were therefore more likely to abuse it.

Is the common cold really that common?

The 'common cold' describes more than 200 viruses that cause a mild infection of the nose, throat and airways. Of these, about half are the more common human rhinoviruses (HRV), the cause of around 40% of colds. So, some 'common colds' are more common than others.

Commonly Speaking

Because there are over 100 known variants of HRV alone, it's impossible to create a cold vaccine. As a result, this frequently received infectious disease has earned its name – most adults will get two to four different colds per year, and children even more. However, once you've had a cold, your body develops antibodies to that strain of the virus – so the more colds you've had, the less likely it is that you will catch a cold in the future.

People over the age of 50 are 50% less susceptible to catching colds than teenagers, and researchers have also found that those who have a healthier lifestyle, more sleep and lower stress levels suffer less from colds than others. A study has also shown that those blessed with longer telomeres (the little 'caps' on your white blood cells that protect chromosomes from damage) are less likely to catch the common cold.

THE COST OF A COLD

Colds are big business, with the US market spending up to $5 billion (£3.9 billion) per year on over-the-counter treatments. But the cost to big business is even more. With nearly 110 million lost days of work and school combined in the United States alone, it's been calculated that $25 billion (£19.5 billion) is lost in productivity every year.

Can you die from a broken heart?

Stress-induced cardiomyopathy – also known as broken heart syndrome – can affect a person with an otherwise healthy heart. Women are more likely to experience the intense chest pain, often misdiagnosed as a heart attack, caused by the surge of stress hormones released during an emotionally stressful event.

Death by Heartache

Another name for the condition is takotsubo cardiomyopathy. *Takotsubo* is a Japanese word for a type of round-bottomed, narrow-necked vessel – the shape of your heart's left ventricle when you're suffering from the syndrome. The left ventricle enlarges and the heart doesn't pump well, leading to an abnormal heartbeat, which, if left untreated, can result in a cardiac arrest. Other symptoms include breathlessness and intense chest pain. There is no specific treatment for takotsubo cardiomyopathy, but a patient may be prescribed medication to ease the symptoms. So, while it is possible that a broken heart could result in death, most people make a full recovery within a few weeks.

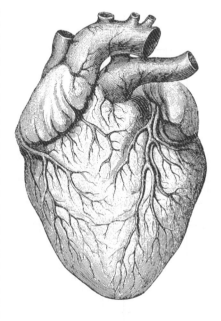

Love You to Death

Three-quarters of those diagnosed with stress-induced cardiomyopathy have recently experienced significant emotional or physical stress – a bereavement, a traumatic break-up or even a happy shock, like winning the lottery. But it is sometimes cited as the reason for elderly partners dying within a short period of each other. Research has shown that there is an increase of risk of death after the hospitalisation of a partner, but that after six months that increase is diminished.

Is chocolate the cure for all ills?

In North America and Europe, people eat a lot of chocolate. While we've come to view that sweet brown candy as a contributor to our expanding waistlines, some scientists are actively encouraging people to indulge their inner chocolate addict – in moderation.

Only the Best

But it's not just any chocolate that will suffice. Cacao beans, from which cocoa is derived, contain antioxidants that boost your immune system. They're packed with more of the good stuff than some so-called super fruits, like acai berries. Natural cocoa powder and dark chocolate are good sources. Unlike its milkier cousin, which contains milk, sugar and cream, a small amount of dark chocolate with at least 65% cacao might do you a world of good.

Treat That Tickly Cough

A 2012 study by the British National Health Service found that persistent coughs were dramatically improved in 60% of patients after they were given a course of theobromine – a chemical derived from cacao beans. Another study showed that the chemical can block the action of the sensory nerves, preventing the cough reflex.

Be Serious

But it's not just a tickly cough that dark chocolate has been shown to help. Here are a few other suspected cacao cures:

- **DEMENTIA** researchers at Harvard University, in the United States, found that two cups of hot chocolate every day could improve mental performance in the elderly. They measured blood flow to the brain – normal levels of which are essential for cognition. In one group, which had impaired blood flow, they noticed an 8% increase after a month.

- **CANCER** While eating chocolate on a regular basis has not been found to prevent cancer, one study showed that pentamer, which is found in chocolate, deactivates proteins that cause cancer cells to divide.
- **DIABETES** Surely diabetics should steer clear of chocolate? Well, apparently not, according to an Italian study that found the flavonoids in dark chocolate could be used to lower blood pressure and increase metabolism of sugar – a protective measure for diabetics.

A Cure Through the Ages

Contemporary scientists are not the first to study the benefits of chocolate. While chocolate's modern history began in the 1500s with the Spanish exploration of South America, cacao beans were a necessary part of ancient civilisations – used for trade and offered up to deities. *The Florentine Codex*, a 1590 document created by a Spanish priest who lived in what is now Mexico, lists several medicinal uses for chocolate, including improvements in asthma, angina and cancer, as well as increased energy and decreased agitation.

HOW MUCH DO WE EAT?

In the United States alone, each person consumes around 5 kilograms of chocolate every year. But 16 of the top 20 chocolate-eating countries are European. In 2015, a *Forbes* survey found that the Swiss eat the most per capita – 9 kilograms, to be exact.

Can twins communicate telepathically?

With their uncanny physical similarities and matching DNA and blood type, twins – especially identical twins – have always fascinated researchers. The study of twins – gemellology – has produced several remarkable results over the years. Yet despite overwhelming anecdotal evidence, no scientific study has found proof of extrasensory perception (ESP) between twins.

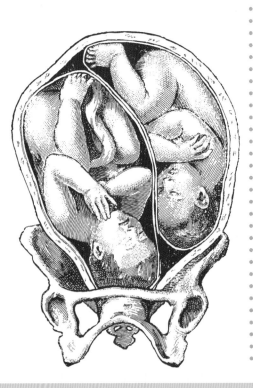

Emotionally Attuned

Twins often make tabloid headlines when one experiences stomach pains as the other is going into labour, or when they are raised apart but end up married to partners with the same name. If they're not reading each other's minds, how are some of these occurrences possible? Some believe the amount of time twins spend together in the womb and in childhood makes them especially attuned to each other's emotions. A 1993 British study of the levels of ESP and thought concordance – the ability to think like each other – in twins, compared to other siblings, found that twins had a marginally higher thought concordance level. But when it came to ESP, there was no evidence that twins had some otherworldly connection. Apparently, they just make better news stories.

A Secret Language

Twins' similar speech patterns and life experiences mean they often finish each other's sentences or each seem to know what the other is going to say next. Telepathy might be unproven in twins, but that doesn't mean they don't have their own special way of communicating. About 40% of twins invent their own 'language' in childhood. This phenomenon is called *cryptophasia*, derived from the Greek for 'secret speech.' Most children develop some of their own words or codes with their siblings, but because of twins' synced-up development, they often come up with a version of their mother tongue with which they can communicate easily. Arguably, most of these 'languages' are not different languages at all, but mispronunciations of their mother tongue that both twins are able to understand – an in-joke. Some twins have created more developed languages of their own, which scientists say tend to follow the same simple structure, no matter where the twins are from or what their native language is.

THE KENNEDY SISTERS

Most twins grow out of using their own language as they learn to speak to their parents and play with other children. In some cases, however, where twins are isolated and receive little outside influence, they have been known to continue their twin-speak into late childhood. Perhaps the most famous case of this was that of the Kennedy sisters. Growing up in 1970s San Diego, United States, Grace and Virginia Kennedy were splashed across the newspapers when it was revealed that, at the age of six, they didn't speak any English, only their own secret language. Childhood convulsions had led their parents to believe they had a mental disability. They were largely confined to the house and looked after by their German grandmother. Their language, it turned out, was a mixture of badly pronounced German and English. After undergoing speech therapy, both girls could speak English, but their language capabilities always lagged behind their peers.

How long ago did cosmetic surgery begin?

Transforming the human body through surgery for aesthetic reasons is nothing new. While surgical procedures today are far more advanced, healers, doctors and even barbers had been performing cosmetic procedures for centuries before the recent surge in popularity for plastic.

Ancient Healers

Plastic surgery gets its name from the Greek word for these types of procedures: *plastikos*, meaning 'moulding'. It's believed early Indian communities widely experimented with shaping parts of the body, particularly the nose, for aesthetic effect. One of the first people to record these cosmetic procedures was an Indian healer known as Sushruta. Scholars believe he lived at some point between 1000 and 600 BCE, and today we know much of his medicine from *Sushruta Samhita*, a 184-page compendium of the healer's teachings, surgeries and medical practices. Among these writings, Sushruta described reconstructive methods for different defects, including rhinoplasty – or nose jobs – using a pedicled forehead flap. After this was published in the *Gentleman's Magazine of Calcutta* in 1794, it began to be used more widely in Europe. This technique is still known today as the Indian flap.

Necro Nip and Tuck

It's believed that Egyptians were averse to performing surgical procedures to alter the face of the living, as they believed your appearance would be the same in the afterlife, and that you should therefore remain as nature intended while you were alive. They did, however, make some modifications to corpses to emphasise prominent features. Ramses II's nose had a small bone and a handful of seeds inserted into it, and bandages were inserted into the cheeks and bellies of other mummies – scholars believe this was to make these features more prominent and therefore recognisable in the afterlife.

THE NAKED TRUTH

In the first century BCE, the Romans were also having a go at fairly advanced surgical procedures. The naked body was widely appreciated in art and culture, and people were comfortable being naked in the public bathhouses. Abnormalities were frowned upon, leading to some men having 'breast' reduction and the removal of scar tissue and the marks of circumcision, according to *De Medicina*, a medical text dating from the time.

No Easy Job

Fifteenth-century rhinoplasties, performed long before the advent of anaesthesia and hygienic hospital practices, were described by Heinrich von Pfolspeundt in his 1460 work, *Buch der Bundth-Ertznei*. A model of the nose was constructed from parchment or leather; this was then positioned on the forearm and traced. The marked area of arm skin was cut around, leaving the bottom of the new nose flap attached. The patient's raised arm would be bound to their head, with the nose flap positioned in place. The patient would then spend up to ten days with their arm attached to their nose before the skin flap was cut and the nostrils constructed.

Can your stomach be embarrassed?

When we blush from embarrassment, it's a result of our body releasing adrenaline as part of the fight-or-flight response. Your heart rate speeds up, and so does your breathing, as you prepare to run from the awkward situation you've just gotten into. But it's not just your face that turns bright red.

Blushing Inside and Out

You might not notice, but there's lots happening on the inside too: your digestive system slows down to redirect energy to your muscles, your pupils dilate to help you take in your surroundings and your blood vessels also expand so that blood can move oxygen around your body more easily. When the veins in your face dilate, more blood flows through them than normal, causing the reddened cheeks we associate with public humiliation. But as your stomach is lined with blood vessels, they are also expanding, blushing in solidarity with your face, even if no one can see.

Social Expectations

Science has struggled to answer the question 'Why do we blush when we're embarrassed?' But many believe

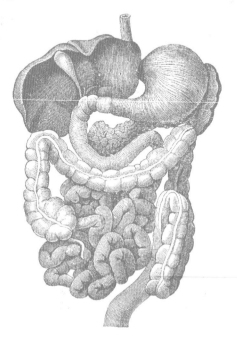

blushing evolved as a way of enforcing social codes. When we blush, others can visibly see we know that what we've said or done might not be seen as acceptable. In a sense, it's a non-verbal apology. This adrenaline-based blushing, which is different from blushing caused by heat, alcohol consumption or arousal, is something that develops in children when they start to become socially aware and conscious of others' feelings, supporting the theory that it developed as a societal function.

Why are barbers' poles red and white?

In many countries, especially in the West, men know where they can go for a short back and sides, a shave, and some manly bonding by the red-and-white barber's pole. Its origins lie in the bloodletting practices of medieval barbers' shops, where getting a cut meant something entirely different.

A Bloody Affair

Bloodletting was a typical treatment for a whole host of conditions in the Middle Ages. From gout and epilepsy to smallpox and even the plague, ordinary people would visit their barber for this treatment, after the Catholic Church banned priests from administering the procedure. A special tool that included a blade, known as a fleam, was used to nick veins or arteries in the arm or neck, and blood would flow into a small brass bowl or wooden cup.

Sometimes leeches were used to let blood instead. In England in 1540, barbers and surgeons became one profession under King Henry VIII, and these 'barber-surgeons' could perform enemas, sell medicine, extract teeth and, of course, cut hair.

Poles, Not Bowls

To advertise their services, barbers would put the brass bowls of their clients' blood in the window. In 1307 a law was passed that forbade this vulgar display, and the barber pole emerged in its place. For the largely illiterate populace, the pole, signifying the red blood and white bandages involved in the practice, was a recognisable symbol of the surgical services the barber offered.

FLEAM (LEFT) AND COLLECTING CUP (RIGHT)

Is it possible to survive rabies?

In 2015, the World Health Organization (WHO) launched a global framework to eliminate human rabies deaths by 2030. The infectious viral disease is present on all continents except for Antarctica, but more than 95% of the tens of thousands of human deaths each year occur in Africa and Asia.

Shocking Symptoms

The name 'rabies' was coined in the 1590s from the Latin word *rabere*, meaning 'to rage'. The Greek philosopher Aristotle wrote of this ancient disease: 'Dogs suffer from the madness. This causes them to become irritable and all animals they bite to become diseased.'

Dog bites are the biggest cause of human rabies deaths, accounting for up to 99% of transmissions, although bats, raccoons, foxes and cats, among others, can also be culprits. Infected animals pass on the disease through their saliva, either by biting, scratching, or a lick to broken skin, the mouth or the eye. After a period of between less than a week and three months, symptoms start to show, including fever and a tingling or burning sensation at the wound site. Then the disease manifests itself in one of two ways. 'Furious rabies' is more common, and the type most people think of when they imagine the disease. Symptoms include hyperactivity, excited behaviour,

hallucinations and a fear of water. Once a person exhibits symptoms, death from drowning in their own spit or blood, inability to breathe or cardiac arrest usually occurs within a couple of days. The other type, 'paralytic rabies', sees the muscles gradually become paralysed until death occurs.

Race Against the Clock

Rabies is vaccine-preventable, although the vaccination is costly, meaning it's largely a disease suffered by poor and vulnerable populations. When a person has been bitten, it's a race against the clock to prevent the disease from entering the central nervous system, even if they've had the vaccine. If the wound is cleaned and the patient is given a potent course of the rabies vaccine, coupled with rabies antibodies if they've not had the vaccine pre-exposure, there is a good chance of survival. Every year, 15 million people receive a post-bite vaccination, which is thought to prevent hundreds of thousands of deaths. But for those who are unable to afford the treatment or don't realise they are infected, the disease is almost always fatal.

The Milwaukee Protocol

In 2004, a 15-year-old girl from Milwaukee, Wisconsin, United States, was bitten by a rabid bat, and although her parents cleaned up the wound, they didn't seek medical treatment. Three weeks later their daughter began to show symptoms of the disease. As it was too late to administer the vaccine or antibodies, doctors at the Children's Hospital of Wisconsin induced a coma, hoping the girl's immune system would build up antibodies to fight the virus, and it worked – she survived. However, in 2014 health officials labelled the 'Milwaukee Protocol' a red herring after it failed to save 26 other patients. They believe the rabies strain that infected the girl might have been a milder, less virulent variant.

Are hats bad for your health?

They're not anymore, but in the 18th and 19th centuries, when headwear was *de rigueur*, makers of felt hats were exposed to large quantities of mercury nitrate. Used in a process called carroting, this substance had a definite impact on people's health.

A Poisonous Place to Work

Both for fashion and function, animal furs were a key material in hat production. Mercury nitrate caused the fur to turn orange, shrink and become easier to remove from the skin, to be made into felt. Repeated exposure saw many workers develop symptoms of mercury poisoning, including emotional instability, memory loss, tremors, speech problems and hallucinations. The British idiom 'mad as a hatter' derives from this unfortunate side effect of working in the millinery industry.

Urea Need to Use the Washroom

Originally, hatters used camel urine to strip the fur from animal skins. The urea component contains nitrogen, which helps to break down the proteins in the fur. Hatters would sometimes replace camel urine with their own, until it was noted that one workman's urine was producing better-quality felt. He was being treated for syphilis with mercury – thus the discovery that mercury nitrate worked wonders on fur.

THE MAD HATTER

One man thought to have suffered particularly from mad hatter syndrome is Boston Corbett – the hat worker turned Unionist who shot President Lincoln's assassin, John Wilkes Booth. He'd castrated himself seven years earlier with a pair of scissors to curb his libido, and ended up in a mental asylum in his 50s, before escaping, never to be seen again.

THE HUMAN BODY

Is your brain bursting with human body trivia?
Try this quiz to see how much you learned.

Questions

1. Who is less likely to catch a cold – a teenager or a 60-year-old?

2. What disease that's most commonly transmitted by a dog bite is named after the Latin *rabere*, meaning 'to rage'?

3. Name an ailment or disease that chocolate has been shown to improve.

4. Cryptophasia is something 40% of twins experience. Is it their own way of walking or talking?

5. What camel-derived liquid did hat workers use to strip the furs of animal skins: saliva, urine or blood?

6. The Black Death was also called the Great Dying – true or false?

7. Blue is the rarest eye colour – true or false?

8. Do studies show that blondes get paid more or less than women with other hair colours?

9. What colours are most barbershop poles?

10. When was the earliest cosmetic surgery recorded? Was it in the period between 1000 and 600 BCE, or in the 15th century?

Turn to page 244 for the answers.

WHY DIDN'T FRIDA KAHLO SMILE IN PHOTOGRAPHS?

ART AND ARCHITECTURE

WHY ARE THE TAJ MAHAL'S TOWERS TILTED?

What happened to the *Mona Lisa's* eyebrows?

While it's the enigmatic smile of Leonardo da Vinci's most well-known subject that's often debated, closer examination of her brow line throws up some interesting discoveries. The *Mona Lisa*'s lack of eyebrows and lashes might be true to the fashion of the era, but more recent investigation has revealed she wasn't always brow-less.

High-Resolution Revelation

In 2007, a French engineer spent 3,000 hours studying 240-megapixel scans of the early 16th-century portrait. Pascal Cotte was able to detect traces of a left eyebrow, invisible to the naked eye, which he believes has gradually eroded due to restoration and cleaning. This would marry with art historian Giorgio Vasari's 1550 description of the painting, in which he wrote: 'The eyebrows, through his having shown the manner in which the hairs spring from the flesh could not be more natural.'

The Layers Beneath

Paintings like the *Mona Lisa*, and the linen canvas or wood they're usually painted on, are susceptible to environmental conditions – humidity, temperature, exposure to direct sunlight – and over time their appearance can change significantly. Old varnish on the original painting, or additional layers applied to help preserve it, yellows and darkens over time, obscuring the light and colours beneath. Art conservationists restore paintings to their original condition with the help of microscopes, chemical analysis and infrared technology. They use techniques such as thinning the varnish and dry cleaning using soft brushes, and rather than water, saliva is sometimes used as a cleaning agent – the warmth and enzyme content act on the lipids and proteins found in dirt.

Why are the Taj Mahal's towers tilted?

In 2004, the Archaeological Survey of India (ASI) dismissed claims that the Taj Mahal's minarets are in danger of collapsing, despite the fact that three of the four towers are tilted by 3.8 to 7.6 centimetres, and the fourth by 21.6 centimetres.

Too Heavy to Handle

The 'tilt' measurements were taken in 1941, when the monument received its first scientific survey, and according to the ASI, which surveys the structure every four years, no structural damage has been found in the more than 70 years since. It's possible that the Taj Mahal's chief architect, Ustad Ahmad Lahauri, designed the towers so they would lean away from the central crypt, where Mumtaz Mahal's casket would reside. Construction began in 1632 and continued for just over two decades – it wasn't uncommon in the 17th century for these architectural behemoths to collapse under their own weight or as the result of an earthquake, so perhaps Lahauri was just being cautious.

A Love to Last for Centuries

Mumtaz Mahal was the third wife of Indian emperor Shah Jahan and mother to 14 of his children. She passed away after complications from childbirth, and not long afterwards her husband oversaw the construction of this lavish tomb – a final gift to his beloved. Around 20,000 people and 2,000 elephants worked to create the structure. When Shah Jahan died in 1666, he was also buried there. Other than the southwest tower's enthusiastic lean, his grave is the only component of the monument that is not completely symmetrical.

Did Van Gogh cut off his own ear?

Self-Portrait with Bandaged Ear (1889) is one of Vincent van Gogh's most recognisable paintings. The bandaged right side of his face has fascinated art historians for decades – some believe he only sliced the earlobe, while others wonder if the wound was not self-inflicted at all.

An Earful of Truth

A letter found in an American archive, and penned by Van Gogh's doctor, Félix Rey, includes a diagram showing how the artist severed almost his entire ear, leaving a small part of the lobe intact. In 2009, a number of historians claimed that fellow painter and house guest Paul Gauguin had sliced off Van Gogh's earlobe in a sword fight. The injury described in Rey's notes, however, is consistent with the theory that a razor blade was used and that it was not an accident.

Downward Spiral

It is clear from his letters that Van Gogh suffered from bouts of depression, and it is thought that he cut off his ear after a dispute with Gauguin (the two men did not reconcile) or because he was unhappy that his brother was to be married. Either way, shortly after the incident Van Gogh was committed to hospital for a time.

In the years since his posthumous rise to fame, doctors have been diagnosing him with conditions such as bipolar disorder, lead poisoning, epilepsy and thujone poisoning caused by the large quantities of absinthe he drank.

The Not-so-Lucky Recipient

For many years it was widely believed that Van Gogh had gifted his severed ear to a sex worker named Rachel who resided in Arles, the French city that was Van Gogh's home for the last year of his life. But recent research has revealed that after the incident on 23 December 1888, Van Gogh made the aural offering to Gabrielle Berlatier, a young woman who worked as a maid at a brothel on Rue du Bout d'Arles. Not long before, she had been bitten by a rabid dog but survived after receiving a newly developed vaccine in Paris,

BANG

where chemist Louis Pasteur had set up a special clinic to study and treat rabies. The cure was expensive, leaving her farming family in debt, which explains why she was working as a maid. She went on to marry and live to an old age, her encounter with the artist kept secret until long after her death.

THE DEATH OF A PAINTER

Van Gogh died in 1890, the year after painting *Self-Portrait with Bandaged Ear*. In the mid-20th century, a 7-mm small-calibre pocket revolver was found buried in the field outside Auvers, a suburb of Paris, where it is believed he shot himself in the chest. The corroded revolver, now owned by a private collector, goes some way towards explaining why the bullet that eventually killed him bounced off his rib – it took him some 30 hours to die from the wound. That type of gun, known as a *Lefaucheux à broche*, was more commonly used for scaring thieves than to kill.

Can you really see the Great Wall of China from the Moon?

The Great Wall is huge, stretching across northern China from Jiayuguan in the west to Shanhaiguan in the east. It is often hailed as the only man-made structure visible from the Moon. In fact, no man-made structures can be seen from the Moon. So why does it have this reputation?

The History Books

Nearly 200 years before humans set foot on the Moon, an English scholar proposed that the wall would be visible from space, while in 1895 journalist Henry Norman wrote that 'The Great Wall of China is, after all, only a wall…' but that 'besides its age it enjoys the reputation of being the only work of human hands on the globe visible from the Moon'. Considering Neil Armstrong, the first man to walk on the Moon, didn't take a look at Earth from the Moon until 1969, these were merely assumptions that captured the public's imagination.

When he returned to Earth, Armstrong was repeatedly asked what he could see from the Moon's surface, which is situated on average 370,000 kilometres from our planet. He said he could make out continents, lakes and splotches of white on blue, but no man-made structures. This has been corroborated by other astronauts since. But still the belief in the wall's impressive scale persists, with many claiming that while it might not be visible from the Moon, it is visible from space.

A Chinese Mission

When Yang Liwei, China's first 'taikonaut', returned from his first mission in 2003, he told reporters he had not seen the wall, much to the country's disappointment. (The term 'taikonaut' is derived from the Chinese word *taikong*, meaning 'space' or 'cosmos' and the Greek word for sailor, *nautes*. It was coined by the English-language media to differentiate between American, Russian and Chinese astronauts.) Other astronauts have claimed to have seen the wall from a low orbit when conditions are favourable, but that the wall's similar colouration to its surroundings makes it hard to spot with the naked eye. Moderate-resolution satellite images can sometimes spot the structure, but they are positioned a mere 705 kilometres above the Earth's surface. And with growing air pollution across China, the wall is becoming harder and harder to see from space.

Disappearing Wall

Soon there might be a lot less of the wall to see from space, with nearly 2,000 kilometres having already disappeared due to erosion and another 1,185 kilometres at risk due to poor conditions – some of which is caused by people stealing bricks to build their houses. However, new parts of the wall are still being discovered, with a research team unearthing in 2011 what they believe to be part of the Great Wall network in southern Mongolia. A report released in 2012 puts its length at 21,196 kilometres.

Why can tourists no longer climb the Statue of Liberty's torch?

At 93 metres tall, and with a sway distance of 15 centimetres in 80-kilometre-per-hour winds, why would anyone want to climb Lady Liberty's torch? Nevertheless, before the Black Tom incident of 1916, it was possible for tourists to access the tip of the flame and savour the view.

In the Dead of Night

On the night of 30 July 1916, guards alerted the Jersey City Fire Department when a fire broke out at the munitions depot on Black Tom Island, not far from Liberty Island. The guards were fleeing the scene when the firemen arrived, and with good reason: they knew that one barge was packed with 50 metric tons of TNT and 69 railcars were filled with thousands of tons of ammunition. These American-made weapons were waiting to be shipped to the Allied forces of World War I. When the fire reached the barge a little after 2 a.m., the series of explosions that followed would have measured 5.5 on the Richter scale. People felt the blast up to 145 kilometres away, including in Philadelphia, and many Manhattan and Jersey residents were thrown from their beds. The statue, including the torch, endured £78,000 worth of damage (equivalent to £1.8 million today) caused by debris from the explosions. Since then, the narrow, 12-metre-long ladder has been closed to the public.

Catching the Culprits

The United States was not in World War I in 1916, but they were supplying the British and French with ammunition – much of which was being shipped from Black Tom Island. German spies had been fairly successful at destroying American ships and their cargo en route to assist the Allies. It was a Slovak immigrant named Michael Kristoff, together with two Germans, who sabotaged the munitions depot that night. After the war, and once investigators had amassed enough evidence to bring about a claim, Germany was ordered to pay £39 million (equivalent to £914 million today) to those who had suffered as a result of Black Tom – the single largest damage claim ever awarded by the Mixed Claims Commission.

Crowning Glory

While it's no longer possible for the public to climb to the dizzying heights of the torch, visitors to Liberty Island can still take in the sights of New York Harbor from the 25 windows of the statue's crown. The tourist attraction is not for the faint-hearted, however, as you have to climb 377 steps to reach the viewing platform.

NEW TORCH, NEW TORCH

The Statue of Liberty is only a nickname – the real name is *Liberty Enlightening the World*. The torch is symbolic of enlightenment, while the seven spikes of the aureole are said to represent the world's seven continents. After the damage sustained to the raised arm and torch in 1916, and years of wear and tear, the original torch was replaced by a new one in 1986, made from copper and covered in 24-karat gold leaf. French sculptor Frédéric Bartholdi's original torch can be admired in the Pedestal Lobby at the base of the statue.

How did M&M's help solve one of the world's greatest art thefts?

There are four versions of Edvard Munch's *The Scream* – two pastels and two paintings. They have become some of the most iconic expressionist works, recognised around the world. No wonder they have been the target of two high-profile robberies in recent years.

Clumsy Collectors

In 2004, two armed robbers walked into a gallery in Oslo, Norway, and in full view of visitors pulled Munch's *The Scream* and *Madonna* from the walls

before making a hasty getaway. Just over two years later, the paintings were found intact by Norwegian police. Bizarrely, this was soon after the confectionery company Mars Inc. offered a reward of two million M&Ms – the equivalent of 40,000 bags – for the safe return of *The Scream*. Little did they know that their publicity stunt would actually encourage someone to come forward – a man serving an unrelated sentence for armed robbery, who apparently hoped to receive conjugal visits, as well as the M&M's, as his reward for helping police to locate the paintings.

A GOLD-MEDAL ATTEMPT

Ten years previously, Pål Enger stole *The Scream* from Oslo's National Gallery. He chose the opening day of the 1994 Winter Olympics, when the police were otherwise engaged, to break in with three accomplices and seize the valuable work, leaving a cheeky note: 'Thousand thanks for the bad security!' The painting was later recovered in a sting operation.

Why did Michelangelo make one of David's hands bigger than the other?

Heralded as one of the greatest sculptures in existence, Michelangelo's *David* is a masterpiece. But despite its exacting recreation of the male form, the statue is out of proportion – the head and hands are unnaturally large. Art historians believe this is because of the work's planned location.

David on High

In 1501, Michelangelo began work on a marble sculpture of David from the biblical story of David and Goliath. Commissioned by the Museo dell'Opera del Duomo for the Cathedral of Florence, the 5-metre statue was to be one of a series to tower 24 metres above ground in the niches of the cathedral's tribunes. It is thought the artist considered the viewer's perspective, making the head and the hands, particularly the right, bigger to emphasise David's intentions as he prepares to fight Goliath. However, the finished statue was so good that it was displayed instead in the Piazza della Signoria, where a replica now stands. The real *David* was relocated to the Galleria dell'Accademia in 1873.

Marble Marvel

Michelangelo was not the first to work on the block of marble. Almost 40 years previously, Agostino di Duccio had planned to sculpt a biblical prophet for the cathedral, but the project was abandoned. Ten years later another artist, Antonio Rossellino, took over the block, but deemed the marble to have too many imperfections, making it hard to work with. In 2005, scientists identified the origins of the marble – the Fantiscritti quarries in Miseglia – and confirmed its mediocre quality.

Why didn't Frida Kahlo smile in photographs?

Considered one of Mexico's greatest modern artists, self-portrait painter Frida Kahlo's life was filled with hardship, tragedy and disappointment, so she'd be easily forgiven for not grinning whenever someone whipped out a camera. However, that familiar stern expression has more to do with orthodontics than anything else – Frida Kahlo really didn't like her teeth.

Pain and Polio

As an artist working to be appreciated in a male-dominated world, Kahlo's sans-smile persona (which shows in all of her self-portraits as well as photographs), coupled with her refusal to conform to gender norms, could have been a creative choice, but she also suffered more than most. She was diagnosed with polio at the age of six, which left her right leg noticeably thinner than her left. She was involved in a tram accident, after which she faced a long road to recovery with a broken spine, pelvis, collarbone and ribs. She suffered from multiple miscarriages and was later forced to terminate three pregnancies. This is thought to be due to the damage sustained to her uterus from the accident. She also suffered from an array of mental illnesses. She underwent 35 operations throughout her life, including the eventual amputation of her right leg below the knee.

Toll on Her Teeth

It's no surprise, then, that she had a bottle-a-day brandy habit, smoked like a chimney and kept a constant supply of candy. All of which can't have done her teeth any favours. She was missing several teeth, including two incisors, which she replaced with two gold false ones. She also had a fancier pair of rose-gold choppers, studded with diamonds, made for special occasions.

DOCTOR KAHLO

If fate hadn't played its part, the world might never have seen the artworks of Frida Kahlo. She had planned to become a doctor, and in 1922 was one of a handful of women enrolled in the prestigious Escuela Nacional Preparatoria. It was after three years of study that she was seriously injured in the tram accident. To pass the three months she spent in a full-body cast, her father set up an easel over the bed, and she began to paint.

Animal Magic

Surely if anything could make you crack a smile, it would be a menagerie of adorable creatures? While Kahlo managed to keep a serious expression, she probably had a whale of a time creating many of her self-portraits that feature animals – including her spider monkey, Fulang-Chang. She also had a trick-performing parrot, a fawn, an eagle, dogs and a number of exotic birds that roamed around her garden.

Has anyone lived in the Eiffel Tower?

In 2016, a vacation rental company transformed a first-floor conference room in the Eiffel Tower into a luxury two-bedroom apartment, and four lucky contest winners got to call the tower home for a night. But there once was a man who could live there as he pleased.

Home on High

Gustave Eiffel was an architect and civil engineer. He built the Eiffel Tower – today one of the world's most-visited tourist attractions – as part of the 1889

Exposition Universelle, which was taking place to celebrate the French Revolution's centennial. It took just over two years to build the tower – an engineering feat of its time. While the original design was only supposed to last for 20 years, Eiffel made sure he would be able to enjoy the views better than anyone. On the third floor, at a height of just over 270 metres, three times the height of Notre Dame Cathedral, was a small apartment. Decorated with dark wood, patterned carpet and wallpaper, and with all the trappings of a typical Parisian home (there was even a grand piano), this was a sanctuary in the sky where Eiffel could study and entertain.

The Price of Privacy

When word got out in Paris about Eiffel's apartment, he was besieged with requests to rent it. Everyone wanted a taste of tower living, but no price was high enough. The lucky few who were invited to attend his private parties were the dignitaries and influential men of the day. Among them was Thomas Edison, the American inventor, who spent time smoking cigars and discussing his inventions with Eiffel. He even presented him

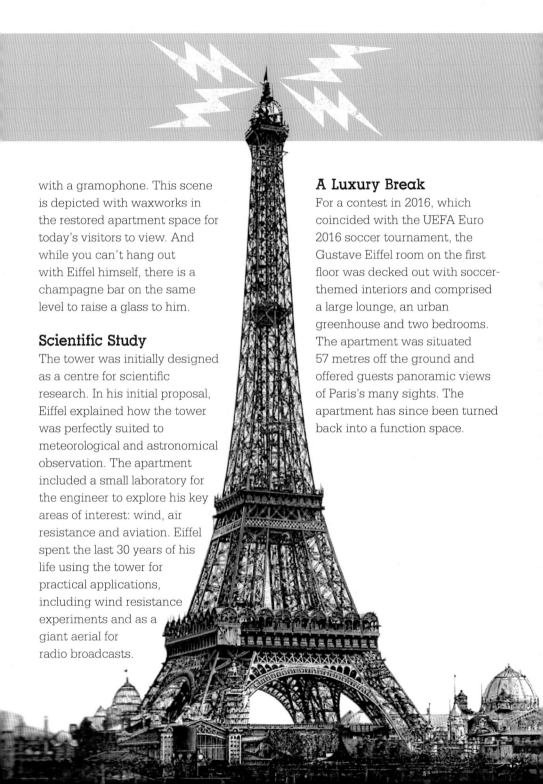

with a gramophone. This scene is depicted with waxworks in the restored apartment space for today's visitors to view. And while you can't hang out with Eiffel himself, there is a champagne bar on the same level to raise a glass to him.

Scientific Study

The tower was initially designed as a centre for scientific research. In his initial proposal, Eiffel explained how the tower was perfectly suited to meteorological and astronomical observation. The apartment included a small laboratory for the engineer to explore his key areas of interest: wind, air resistance and aviation. Eiffel spent the last 30 years of his life using the tower for practical applications, including wind resistance experiments and as a giant aerial for radio broadcasts.

A Luxury Break

For a contest in 2016, which coincided with the UEFA Euro 2016 soccer tournament, the Gustave Eiffel room on the first floor was decked out with soccer-themed interiors and comprised a large lounge, an urban greenhouse and two bedrooms. The apartment was situated 57 metres off the ground and offered guests panoramic views of Paris's many sights. The apartment has since been turned back into a function space.

Why did Andy Warhol paint Campbell's Soup tins?

Andy Warhol's iconic *Campbell's Soup Cans* (1982) has become symbolic of the 1960s pop art movement, and the man himself. Whether the painting is viewed as a comment on burgeoning American consumerism or mass manufacturing, one thing's for sure – Andy Warhol loved Campbell's Soup.

Twenty Years of Slurping

Warhol famously said: 'I used to drink it. I used to have the same lunch every day, for twenty years.' He was talking,

of course, about Campbell's Soup, the subject matter he chose to work with in 1962. He traced projections onto canvas and meticulously painted the outlines to reflect the lithograph printing style of the original labels. While the 32 canvases might look identical at a glance, there is one for every flavour available that year, including Oyster Stew, Chicken 'N Dumplings, and Hot Dog Bean. Five of the paintings sold individually for $100, but the gallery owner bought them back when he realised the paintings made more sense as a group. He eventually sold them to New York's MoMA in 1996 for over $15 million.

THE SOUPER DRESS

This wasn't Warhol's only dalliance with the famous brand of soup; he produced a number of other works featuring the tins. He also printed his designs on paper dresses, which were worn by New York socialites. Wanting to cash in on their newfound cool appeal, in 1965 Campbell's Soup produced the Souper Dress – their own paper dress, which customers could buy for a dollar and two soup tin labels.

ART AND ARCHITECTURE

Filled to the brim with artefacts and arty facts? Get to grips with what you've read with this little quiz.

Questions

1. The Taj Mahal was a tomb for Emperor Shah Mahan's favourite elephant – true or false?

2. Which iconic tower was built for the 1889 Exposition Universelle in Paris?

3. What are the seven spikes on the Statue of Liberty's crown thought to represent – the seven continents or the seven deadly sins?

4. Saliva is sometimes used to restore oil paintings instead of water – true or false?

5. Which part of his body did Van Gogh famously cut off?

6. Why can't you see the Great Wall of China from the Moon?

7. How many versions are there of Edvard Munch's *The Scream*?

8. What brand of soup did Andy Warhol famously paint – Heinz or Campbell's?

9. Michelangelo's *David* is based on David Beckham – true or false?

10. Which country was Frida Kahlo from: Canada, the United States or Mexico?

Turn to page 245 for the answers.

CAN ANY PLANTS CALL FOR HELP WHEN THEY'RE BEING EATEN?

WHY DO WE KISS UNDER THE MISTLETOE?

HOW DO PIGEONS FIND THEIR WAY HOME?

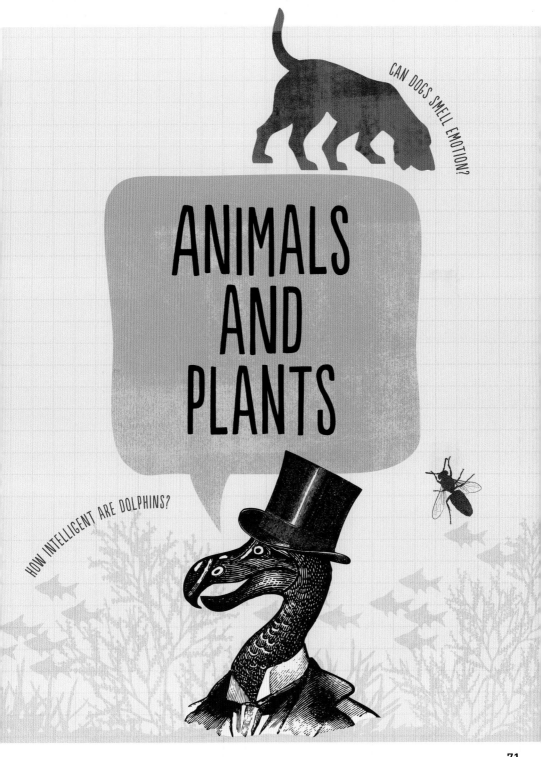

CAN DOGS SMELL EMOTION?

ANIMALS AND PLANTS

HOW INTELLIGENT ARE DOLPHINS?

What's the most painful insect sting?

QUESTION 34 QUESTION

Only three insects have had their sting rated '4' on the Schmidt Index: the warrior wasp, the tarantula hawk wasp and – most excruciating – the bullet ant, the pain of which is described as akin to walking over flaming coals with a 7-centimetre rusty nail stuck in your heel.

The Schmidt Index

American entomologist Justin Orvel Schmidt began rating the pain caused by insect stings after experiencing a number of painful ones himself in the course of his research into Hymenoptera – stinging ants, wasp, and bees. His Schmidt Sting Pain Index, published in 1984, has been updated twice since – Schmidt has now been stung by some 150 different species.

The five-point index ranges from 0 to 4, with 0 defined as the feeling of being stung by an insect that cannot penetrate human skin and 4 an intensely painful sting. The bullet ant, *Parponera clavata*, native to the tropical forests of Central America, is the world's largest ant species. Its venom contains poneratoxin, which causes sweats, nausea and extreme pain. Bullet ants are generally not aggressive unless provoked – the venom evolved as a way to protect their colonies.

WHY DO INSECTS STING?

Bee, wasp and ant stings are actually adapted from parts of their egg-laying anatomy, so usually only females sting. They use their sting as a weapon, to hunt and kill prey, protect their nests and defend their lives against other predators. Hymenoptera are all descendants of a wasp-like stinging ancestor that existed over 100 million years ago, so they're obviously doing something right.

BULLET ANT

Why do elephants have such big ears?

While all mammals have their evolutionary oddities, the elephant stands out for its size, its nose and its large floppy ears. Unlike the auricular appendages of other warm-blooded animals, the elephant's ears are supersized. The reason? Their ears are how they stay cool.

Hot Stuff

The sheer size of an elephant means it produces a vast amount of metabolic heat. An elephant's skin alone cannot release that heat quickly enough, and those large, flat ears are essential. They're tightly packed with veins through which hot blood can pump and release the heat. However, this will only happen if the surrounding air is colder than 38°C, which isn't always the case in their natural habitat. To help with the cooling process, elephants seek out shade and never stray too far from water (although desert-dwelling elephants can go several days without it), often spraying water over their ears with their trunk to keep them wet. They also flap their ears, generating their own cooling breeze.

Horses for Courses

Where elephants live in cooler climates, such as India, their ears are noticeably smaller. Mammoths, which lived in the tundra regions of Siberia, had fur and thick layers of fat to keep them warm, and – unlike their descendants – really small, furry ears.

Why do flamingos stand on one leg?

Debate still rages about why flamingos spend much of their time – sometimes up to four hours at a stretch – balancing their body weight on one long, spindly leg. Suggested explanations range from camouflage among the surrounding reeds to just being more comfortable. However, it's widely agreed that it's likely to do with staying warm.

Keeping Cosy

Comparative psychologists Matthew Anderson and Sarah Williams observed that flamingos are more likely to stand on one leg while wading than when they're on land. They believe the reason is thermoregulation: when the flamingo is in the water, it loses more body heat by keeping both legs submerged, hence the balancing act.

Left- or Right-Headed?

When Anderson and Williams set out to research the flamingo, they'd initially hoped to learn whether the bird has a preference for the side of its body it uses for specific tasks. They noticed that while flamingos do have a preference for which side they rest their heads (most rest their head to the right, in the same way most humans are right-handed), they don't seem to mind which side does the legwork. They also noted that the birds that went against the grain and rested their head on the left were likely to be more aggressive towards other birds.

Reflex Action

Scientists in New Zealand may have found another reason entirely for the flamingo's one-legged lifestyle. They think the behaviour might be more to do with a natural reflex than the temperature of the water. They found that it's likely flamingos share a primitive ability with whales and dolphins, which are able to shut down just part of their brain when they sleep in the water, to prevent them from drowning. If so, the action of tucking the leg up could be a result of them becoming drowsy – a natural reflex in line with how the bird would normally lower itself to the ground for sleep. The researchers believe this half-awake state allows them to rest while staying vigilant to predators.

Pink Pool Party

With their bright pink plumage, flamingos are one of the most recognisable birds in the world. But they don't start out that way – flamingo chicks have grey feathers. They develop their distinctive hue from their diet of algae and shrimp. These foods are rich in carotenoids, which are broken down in the liver into pigment molecules, and absorbed by fatty deposits in the feathers, legs and even bill. This helps to explain the variance in colour of flamingos in different parts of the world. Where flamingos eat more algae, such as in the Caribbean, they are a richer, deeper colour; but where their diet is made up of small creatures that feed on algae, they're usually a lighter pink.

Can dogs smell emotion?

Dogs' noses are wondrous things. Their acute sense of smell enables them to be trained to detect bombs and drugs, and find earthquake survivors. But it also makes them fine-tuned to human emotions, strengthening the bond between dog and owner and helping them serve as therapeutic companions to those in distress.

A Nose of Two Halves

Dogs have a unique nasal system. Unlike our rather basic noses, where breathing in and out occurs through the same part of the nostrils, dogs' noses have a clever slit at the sides, where the air passes out. This means they can build up the concentration of a particular scent by drawing more odour molecules into their nose more quickly. Inside their nose there are two

separate areas: one for breathing and one for smelling. The smelling region features hundreds of millions of olfactory cells, compared to a human's meagre ten million. These cells are what help to send electrical signals to the brain.

Sense of Smell

It could be said that dogs are wired to smell. The portion of the canine brain dedicated to smell is significantly larger than the relative area used in a human brain. The damp, spongy surface area of the nose works to draw air molecules in. This, combined with the fact that dogs can smell through both nostrils separately, helping them to determine the direction a scent is coming from, makes for a nose of epic capabilities. It can detect and interpret smells at concentrations 100 million times lower than a human can.

How about Hormones?

On top of their super-sensitive sniffing skills, dogs are gifted with a particularly astute vomeronasal organ, which sits above the roof of their mouth. It is also known as the Jacobson's organ, after its discoverer, anatomist Ludvig Levin Jacobson. Its primary function is to detect pheromones – chemical compounds, often without any discernible scent, that transmit signals between organisms of the same species. They help dogs to identify both potential mates and hostile threats from other animals. Studies have shown that dogs can also pick up on other animals' pheromones, including those of humans. These pheromone scents can help a dog detect a person's gender and age, and whether a woman is pregnant.

Unfortunately, research into human pheromones is severely lacking. For example, while scientists have been able to identify two pheromones, androstenone and androstenol, that attract fertile female boars to their male counterparts, they've not been able to isolate a human equivalent. There is significant evidence from studies, such as babies being able to smell breast milk and adults being able to determine whether a person is anxious or not by the smell of their sweat, that shows our pheromones give out signals, but apparently dogs are a lot more adept at reading them than we are.

How do pigeons find their way home?

Humans have relied on pigeons' homing instincts for sport and communications since ancient Greek and Roman times, yet we're still not able to say definitively *how* they navigate. We do know, however, that pigeons have adapted to the modern age, using sights and smells to help them complete their journeys.

Road Sense

There are a number of prevailing theories about how pigeons manage to return home to their loft when released hundreds of kilometres away. The

instinct to return to a mate, a nest and a known food source is strong, but is it strong enough to enable champion racing pigeons to navigate up to 970 kilometres in a day at speeds of over 110 kilometres per hour? Research points to their use of low-frequency sound waves to mentally map their environment, the position of the sun and the Earth's magnetic field. A ten-year study by the University of Oxford found that pigeons use our roads and motorways to navigate, even if these don't follow the most direct route. In the study, some pigeons even turned at junctions.

Follow Your Nose

Researchers have tried snipping nerves in pigeons' olfactory systems to see how much their sense of smell affects their navigational nous. While it's unlikely these birds follow their noses entirely, this did prove detrimental to their ability to get around. A study in China saw 415 racing pigeons make their way back more quickly in areas with high air pollution, possibly because the stronger scent signals in polluted air help the pigeons to map their location more easily.

Sheer Magnetism

The Earth's magnetic field plays a role in animal navigation beyond the pigeon loft. Biologists have found evidence that migratory birds, sea turtles and lobsters all use it in some way to find food sources, home or temperate climes. Blindfolded pigeons are still able to find their lofts, a good indicator that they don't just rely on the position of the sun and visual cues.

The planet's magnetic field is strongest at the poles and weakest at the equator. Research undertaken over many years by Dr Charles Walcott at Cornell University, New York, points towards the idea that pigeons can measure the strength and angle of this field, correcting course as need be. In one study, magnetised coils with their polarity reversed were placed on the birds' heads. When released far from home, the pigeons flew in the opposite direction to their home. He also found tiny amounts of magnetic iron ore inside the upper portion of pigeons' beaks, although the effect and purpose of these deposits are not known.

THE KING'S ANGELS

Carrier pigeons were used by some of the world's most significant ancient civilisations to relay messages – from the Egyptians letting neighbouring cities know about the state of the Nile to the Romans finding out the results at the latest Olympic Games. Descended from the rock dove, these messengers were known as 'King's Angels' by Arabs, who used the birds to hear news from all corners of the empire.

What is the world's largest single organism?

How do you measure large? Tallest? Longest? Heaviest? If you consider weight alone, the blue whale – the world's largest animal – can tip the scale at 200 metric tons. Pretty big, you might think. But it pales in comparison to the heaviest single organism: a tree with the nickname Pando, Latin for 'I spread'.

The Root of the Matter

Made up of 47,000 tree trunks, and spanning 43 hectares of the Wasatch Mountains in Utah, United States, is a quaking aspen that holds the title for the world's heaviest organism. Sharing a single root system and a unique set of genes, it is believed to weigh an estimated 5.9 million kilograms. That's significantly heavier than the world's largest giant sequoia, which weighs in somewhere around 2 million kilograms.

While most trees reproduce using sexual reproduction (either through a male tree producing pollen in its flowers, which is then used to fertilise the flowers in a female tree, or a single tree fulfilling the roles of both sexes), some species, like the male quaking aspen, use vegetable reproduction. The tree sends out roots horizontally underground, up to distances of 30 metres. Shoots grow vertically from these roots, becoming stems and developing into new tree trunks, the tree thereby cloning itself many times over. Because of this connectedness, when a single stem dies the entire organism is affected by a hormonal imbalance. Multiple stem deaths lead to a huge increase in new stems as the tree attempts to make up the numbers.

Fabulous Fungus

Little things can be big too. That is never truer than in the case of a particular honey fungus in the Blue Mountains of Oregon, United States. Responsible for the deaths of dozens of trees in the Malheur National Forest, *Armillaria solidipes* spreads below ground in search of new hosts. Above ground, its honey-hued mushrooms reveal its presence. In 1998, researchers found that 61 trees had been killed by the same clonal colony of the fungus, despite being spaced nearly 4 kilometres apart. They calculated that the fungus covered an area of over 9 square kilometres and believed it to be somewhere between 1,900 and 8,650 years old, making it one of the world's oldest organisms, too.

BIG BLUE

It's hard to fathom the size of a blue whale. They can grow to lengths of 30 metres (roughly the height of a ten-story building) and their hearts alone can weigh as much as a car. Their astonishing size means their blowhole spray can reach heights of 9 metres and they can call to each other even if they're 1,600 kilometres apart. In the water, their biggest competition in the size department comes from the sperm whale, known to reach nearly 24 metres in length.

How intelligent are dolphins?

The encephalisation quotient of dolphins – their brain size in relation to their average body size – is second only to humans, leading to the much-repeated statement that they are one of the most intelligent creatures on Earth. But how is this intelligence measured, and what exactly do they use it for?

What Is Intelligence?

There are many ways to define intelligence, and even more ways to measure it. When people talk about how smart dolphins are, they're usually comparing dolphin intelligence to that of humans, making comparisons between the way dolphins socialise and communicate and the way we do.

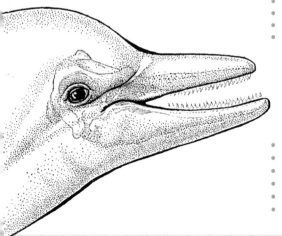

However, some researchers have argued that while dolphins score highly on many tests involving symbol use and social recognition, similarly to great apes and corvids (the family of birds that crows and magpies belong to), and they communicate via echolocation, when it comes to other metrics, such as food calls and alarms, there are many other species that score very highly, including chickens. This has led some researchers to argue that it's not that the dolphin is a standout species, but that we underestimate the capabilities of other animals.

Teething Problems

Around 34 million years ago, dolphins' ancestors, with their large wolf-like teeth, were thrashing around in the water. These predators were faced with a significant period of oceanic cooling, causing a dramatic change in food supplies, forcing them to evolve in a way that suited their new environment. As a result, the dolphin developed a much larger brain, capable of communicating by echolocation, with smaller, peg-like teeth arranged in a configuration that acts as an antenna. Their teeth are not used for chewing, as they swallow their food whole, but

for gripping objects and as defensive weapons. Rather than being solitary hunters, dolphins were now able to work together to hunt large groups of fish.

Tools and Tricks

Dolphins' ability to create complex social networks has been key to their survival. Each social network develops its own unique hunting strategies and behaviours, suited to the climate and environment it's in. For example, in Shark Bay off the Australian coast, some bottlenose dolphins place sea sponges on their beaks for protection from the sharp coral, making it much easier to dig up the seabed for fish; while off the coast of Florida, United States, one dolphin will swim fast in a circle to stir up the sand below, creating a net. It then alerts the other dolphins to line up to catch the bounty as the fish try to escape.

It's All Relative

These highly intelligent animals also have a complex social structure that even a human would struggle to keep track of. Male dolphins are known to form pairs or trios that they can stick with for decades. They work together in these small groups to court and guard females. But when they face confrontation with other dolphin groups, they team up with other pairs or trios, known as second-order alliances, to steal females and defend their own.

Can parrots really talk?

Parrots are social creatures, and when they live in captivity or are kept as pets, they attempt to communicate with their human companions – not by talking, as it might appear, but by mimicking the sounds made by those around them.

Pretty Polly

There are nearly 400 known parrot species, many of which are able to imitate the calls of other birds, and they are often regarded as some of the smartest winged creatures in the animal kingdom. There are some African grey parrots, for example, that have been able to repeat over a thousand different words. However, much research points to the fact that that is all they're doing – imitating the sounds they hear. In the wild, these highly intelligent creatures can have long lifespans and need to learn the calls and sounds made by their family and flock to create social cohesion. Of all the parrot species, budgerigars (also known as common pet parakeets) are the most likely to mimic human sounds and repeat them on cue – they can also recreate the sounds of doorbells and telephones!

Song Nuclei

Parrots are not the only bird type to have mimicking capabilities. Indian mynah birds and northern mockingbirds are just two other species that rely on this instinct for survival. Their ability to imitate has been

attributed to a 'song nucleus' in the brain. This group of interconnected neurons is responsible for synchronising singing and learning. Parrots can be so attuned to each other's calls, they even have local dialects that help them to recognise where another bird is from, which could be crucial for avoiding enemies and selecting mates.

A Life of Learning

Alex was an African grey parrot who lived to the age of 31. Most of his years were spent as part of a study conducted by Dr Irene Pepperberg, a comparative psychologist at Harvard and Brandeis Universities in the United States. She picked Alex up from a pet shop when he was one and began to teach him to communicate using basic expressions. One primary method she used was to award a trainer – for example, a grape – when Alex did the thing she wanted him to do. Alex soon cottoned on to the game. He was able to describe objects, shapes, colours and materials; he could perform simple arithmetic; and he understood some basic concepts. Although Alex never developed the logic capabilities that most infant children pick up early in life, his capacity to learn far surpassed expectations, leading to continued research in the field. His final words to Dr Pepperberg when she put him in his cage for the last time were: 'You be good, see you tomorrow. I love you.'

QUESTION 42 QUESTION

Why don't giraffes get head rushes?

With a 60-centimetre-long heart, weighing up to 11 kilograms, and the highest known blood pressure of any mammal, you'd think simple tasks like taking a sip of water would make a giraffe quite woozy. But these impressive creatures have a unique cardiovascular system that renders those 5-metre head raises a breeze.

What Is a Head Rush?

The woozy feeling, often called a head rush, is caused by the effects of lowered blood pressure when you move too quickly from a seated or horizontal position to a vertical position. The body has built-in mechanisms to increase blood pressure, moving more blood from your legs and feet up to your head when you stand up, but if this doesn't happen effectively enough, you will feel light-headed.

Big-Hearted Creature

While a person's head is positioned about 30 centimetres from their heart, a giraffe's can be 2 metres away. Their enlarged hearts are designed to counteract this distance and the effects of gravity with power, pumping 73 litres of blood per minute. This exceptionally high blood pressure is great for when the giraffe is bolt upright, feeding from the tops of trees, but what about when it bows down for a quick drink? Valves positioned in the main neck veins automatically close when the giraffe bends down, reducing the amount of blood travelling to the head. These veins grow thicker and stronger over time and have an elastic quality that enables them to expand and contract to accommodate the sudden changes in blood flow.

Soak It Up

The final flourish of this anatomical marvel is a sponge-like web of veins at the base of the giraffe's brain, which helps to absorb and divert as much blood as possible when the head is lowered. Then, when the giraffe raises its head, the veins are able to quickly restore blood flow to the brain so the animal doesn't get light-headed on its quick ascent.

GIRAFFES
IN SPACE

Giraffe physiology has been studied by NASA scientists to help them reduce the effects of a weightless environment on astronauts' blood vessels. In a similar way to space travellers, who spend most of the time with reduced blood pressure in their lower limbs, foetal giraffes' legs don't face much gravitational pull in the womb, but as soon as they're born, things are very different. In the 1980s, scientists recorded how baby giraffes, which are normally on their feet 30 minutes after birth in the wild, quickly build their own gravity-defying suit. The blood vessels and skin of their legs thicken, so blood cannot pool there. These natural compression socks were instrumental in the development of NASA's Lower Body Negative Pressure Device, a treadmill contraption that applies negative pressure to the lower body while exercising in space, helping to prevent the loss of cardiovascular function and muscle.

Can any plants call for help when they're being eaten?

Plants have powerful defence mechanisms to protect them from predators. For example, when certain plants are bitten by insects, they detect toxic chemicals and in response release a chemical of their own, toxic to the insect. But some plants need allies in the animal kingdom to help them defend against attack.

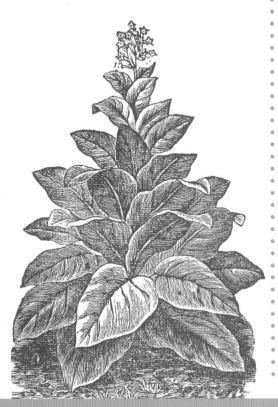

The Secret Life of Plants

Many studies have been made of *Nicotiana* species, otherwise known as tobacco plants. As their seeds can lie dormant for over a century, they have to be extremely resilient and adaptive to their environment, never knowing what the next threat will be. Caterpillars that decide to tuck into one had better watch out, because their saliva causes the plant to produce airborne chemicals that attract a parasitic wasp. This wasp likes to lay its eggs inside the caterpillars; the larva feeds on the caterpillar as it grows, eventually killing it. This mutually beneficial relationship works out well for both the plant and the wasp (the caterpillar, not so much).

Call of the Wild

Corn, tobacco and cotton plants all send out chemicals to attract specific parasitic wasps that feed on the caterpillar species that attack them. Studies have found that commercial tobacco plants go one better by trying to minimise their chances of attack both day and night by making the most of whichever insects are up and about. Parasitic wasps hunt during the day, so plants call them for help when the sun's

up, but when the plants are under attack at night, they emit a different chemical blend that deters nocturnal moths from laying eggs. This helps to keep the hungry caterpillar population down when the plant is most vulnerable.

Talking Trees

Some plants, not content with conversing with the insect world, are able to communicate with other leafy species, too. While the study of plant communication is relatively recent, initial research looked into whether plants were capable of signalling, intentionally or not, to their own kind and other species, warning other plants of impending danger.

A 1980s study, 'The Secret Life of Plants', became a huge sensation when it claimed that damaged maple and poplar trees released chemical cues that seemed to increase defences in their undamaged neighbours. Over the years, research has been extended to a number of other plants, and food scientists are harnessing this new information to change the way crops

are farmed. In East Africa, fields of maize are constantly under attack from stem-borer caterpillars. But if molasses grass is grown alongside the maize, the attacks are less catastrophic. The grass attracts a wasp that keeps the caterpillar population under control.

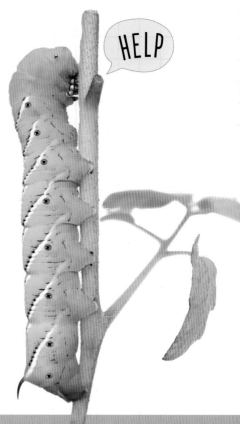

Why do we kiss under the mistletoe?

It's a tradition in many parts of the world to hang mistletoe in a doorway during the festive season. Any pair caught underneath it is supposed to kiss. But where does this ritual stem from, and what does it have to do with the white-berried plant?

The Stuff of Legends

Mistletoe became part of Christmas celebrations in third-century Europe, but the root of its mythical magic comes from the Norse god Balder. Favoured by all the gods, and particularly his own mother, the goddess Frigg, an oath was taken by all the creatures, objects and elements that they would not hurt Balder. Jealous of this new power, the trickster god Loki set out to find something that could hurt him – and he stumbled across mistletoe, so small and insignificant that Frigg had overlooked it. A dart containing the poisonous plant killed Balder, leaving his mother so devastated it was declared that mistletoe would never harm again and she would kiss anyone who passed under it. In the legend, her tears formed into the white berries of the plant.

PARASITIC POUT

While mistletoe conjures images of romance and awkward festive encounters, the plant itself is actually a parasite, stealing nutrients from a host plant to survive. The scientific name for the American mistletoe genus is *Phoradendron*, Greek for 'thief of the tree'.

Why do crocodiles swallow stones?

While the typical crocodile diet would turn most human stomachs – frogs, molluscs and rotting carcasses, anyone? – it's the side order of stones that is truly unappealing. Crocs are one of a few creatures in the animal kingdom to swallow stones. And they don't do this by accident.

Digestive Dirt

When stones are swallowed, they are known as gastroliths. And there are a few reasons crocodiles do this – these rocky ready meals are really rather useful.

First, they can aid a crocodile's digestion. Rocks in the stomach help to grind up food, which is particularly helpful when you're not taking the time to chew. Crocodiles have been known to eat large animals whole, so the gastroliths help to break down the bones and shells of their prey. Some scientists also think the rocks help the crocodile to feel fuller when prey is scarce.

Weighty Meal

Crocodiles spend a significant amount of time underwater, or with only their eyes and nostrils visible, stalking their prey. The added weight of 4 or 5 kilos from gastroliths can help to weigh them down under the water. Some scientists think the increase in body weight is not significant enough to affect buoyancy, but that the rocks have more of a stabilising effect, so the croc is less likely to roll from side to side in the water.

YUM...

Do sunflowers really follow the sun?

Sunflowers take their name rather seriously. When it comes to sun-worshipping, they do it better than any of us. Young sunflowers start their day facing east as the sun rises and track it all the way to the west. Overnight they make the slow journey back, to begin again.

Growing Strong

According to a team of researchers at the University of California, Davis, United States, young sunflowers follow the sun because of the way they grow. This sun-tracking, also known as heliotropism, is caused by sunflower genes that respond to light and the plant's built-in 24-hour biological processes cycle, known as a circadian rhythm. During the day, the east side of the plant grows more, elongating it towards the west, while at night it's the west's turn to grow, orienting it back. When researchers forcibly prevented plants from turning to face the sun, they displayed significantly less mass and leaf surface area.

Easterly Blooms

Adult sunflowers tend to settle facing east. East-facing flowers warm up faster, and warmer flowers attract more bees, which in turn means more pollination. Researchers compared east-facing flowers to west-facing ones, and found that the former attracted five times more pollinators. So how do they get into an easterly position? As a plant matures and its growth slows down, this built-in circadian clock ensures that the plant reacts more strongly to the early morning light than the afternoon light, so it gradually stops moving westward.

ANIMALS AND PLANTS

Think you've got the birds and bees all figured out?
Make sure you're top of the class with this quick quiz.

Questions

1. Which long-necked animal has special valves in its neck veins to prevent it from getting a head rush?

2. What is the bullet ant best known for: its speed or its painful sting?

3. A dog's Jacobson's organ would be found in its tail – true or false?

4. What is the world's largest animal?

5. Parakeets are a species of which type of bird, known for its mimicking ability?

6. Crocodiles swallow stones to weigh them down – true or false?

7. In relation to their average body size, are dolphins' brains large or small?

8. What makes flamingos pink?

9. Which direction do adult sunflowers tend to face?

10. Pigeons use roads to navigate and find their way home – true or false?

Turn to page 245 for the answers.

WHY WAS IT SO HARD TO POISON A ROMAN EMPEROR?

HOW DID MAYAN PARENTS MAKE SURE THEIR BABIES WERE AT THE HEIGHT OF FASHION?

WHAT SPORTS DID THEY PLAY AT THE ANCIENT GREEK OLYMPICS?

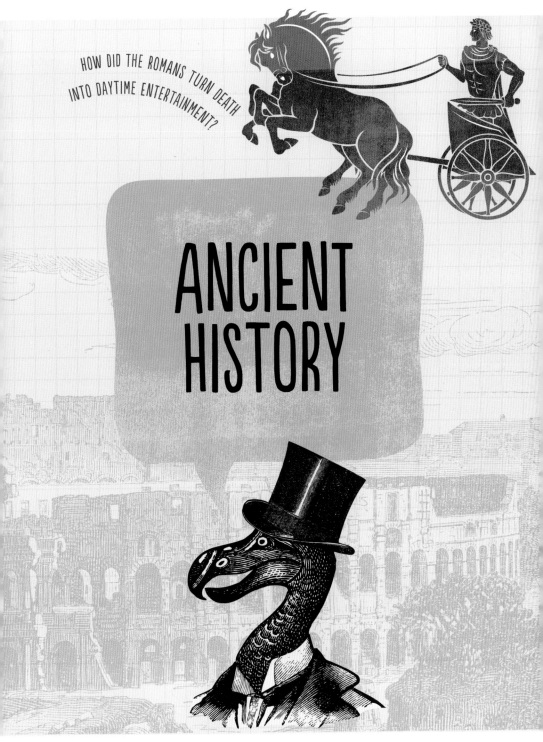

HOW DID THE ROMANS TURN DEATH INTO DAYTIME ENTERTAINMENT?

ANCIENT HISTORY

How did the Incas build Machu Picchu so high up?

Set in a tropical mountain forest in the Amazonian Andes, 2,400 metres above sea level, Machu Picchu is a 15th-century architectural marvel. It might seem odd to choose to build a stone fortress at such a high altitude – but nestled at the top of that mountain was a quarry of white granite.

Stone on Stone

The Historic Sanctuary of Machu Picchu, a UNESCO World Heritage Site, was built in the classical Inca style of the period. The whole site covers 32,592 hectares, and centres around the structure at the top of the mountain, La Ciudadela – the citadel. The entire complex was meticulously planned before the first piece of granite was cut from the quarry. The quarry wasn't the only reason the site was selected. Its sacred relevance (the Incas believed it was close to the sun god), spectacular views and nearby natural spring, which served as the community's water supply, all played a part.

Magic Steps

Key to the build's success were the city's foundations. The Incas knew the site had to be able to withstand high rainfall – 2 metres every year – and the weight of the planned structures. A deep foundation was dug out for over 600 terraces, most of which were hidden underground. Retaining walls that leaned inwards provided stability for the terrace system, preventing the city from sliding off the mountain. The walls were filled in with layers of large rocks, smaller rocks, sandy gravel and topsoil, allowing rainwater and groundwater to drain through the

terraces. A typical terrace was built about 2 metres high by 3 metres wide. Working like claws to cling to the mountain, they are the reason the site remains so well preserved despite 400 years of neglect. The terraces also provided a place to grow crops for the isolated community.

Rock Around the Clock

Hundreds of thousands of stones were used to build around 200 structures, including several temples, 600 terraces, 16 fountains and thousands of steps. The stones, which came from a number of nearby quarries, weighed up to 13 metric tons. Without the modern benefit of motorised equipment, or even animals or wheeled carts to move the stone for them, the Incas made ingenious use of leverage, placing logs beneath the rocks and pushing them in unison. They also had ramps made from earth, which they could move into place to help push a stone uphill. The Incas had no iron tools – the precise stonework, which rivals modern production methods, was achieved using a hammer stone to carve the rock. It is thought that a wooden-wedge technique was also used to break up larger rocks. Holes would be drilled into the rock and wet wood inserted; the water in the wood would then freeze and expand, splitting the rock apart. And the Incas didn't use any kind of mortar to hold the wall together. The rocks were cut accurately, often with indentations that would lock together.

Why was it so hard to poison a Roman emperor?

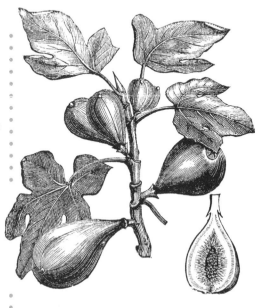

Since the age of a great Roman enemy, Mithridates VI Eupator, King of Pontus (120–63 BCE), emperors routinely poisoned themselves to build up immunity to the very real threat of assassination, making it very difficult to kill them by this method.

Pick Your Poison

The Romans lived in murderous times – mass poisonings were not unheard of – and no one was more at risk than the rich and powerful rulers. While animal and mineral poisons were occasionally used, such as cantharidin from beetles or mercury and arsenic, the most common way to bring about a rival's death was through vegetable poisons. These included belladonna alkaloids, found in deadly nightshade, which causes hallucinations and convulsions; aconite from wolf's bane, a large dose of which could bring about sudden death; and hemlock, which attacks the central nervous system, causing seizures and respiratory failure.

Recipe to Rule By

Mithridates was considered one of the greatest kings of his time, reported to speak 25 languages. He had a keen interest in medicine and developed several antidotes, which tended to contain unusual ingredients such as duck blood. One antidote, made up of a number of poisonous substances, took his name and became popular with those who succeeded him: mithridatium. While researchers are uncertain exactly what the antidote would have contained, one recipe recorded by Roman author Pliny included two nuts, two figs, 20 leaves of the herb rue and a pinch of salt. Reportedly, 'He who took this fasting would be immune to all poison for that day.'

How did the Aztecs keep fit?

The Aztecs, or Mexica as they called themselves, lived in what is now Central America, and are best known for their impressive architecture and for being wiped out by smallpox. But their highly developed culture and customs included mandatory schooling for children, keeping tax records, intricate art and their own popular sport.

Game of Two Hoops

When the Mexica settled somewhere new, one of the first things to be constructed was a *tlachtli* – a court with two facing walls, where people played *ullamaliztli*. On each wall was a ring with six pegs on either side. Players on two teams would then attempt to get a rubber ball, called an *ulli*, through the ring. Points were awarded for knocking out the pegs, and the team to get the ball through their ring first was the winner. This was notoriously difficult, as the ball could only come into contact with players' knees, forearms, head, feet, hips, buttocks and elbows; their hands, calves and even the floor were out of play. In parts of Mexico a game called *ulama*, which bears many similarities to this ancient sport, is still played today.

Roll the Stones

A less energetic pastime was *patolli*. Similar to contemporary dice games like pachisi and ludo, with its cross-shaped board, red bean counters and stone die, this was a game of chance and skill popular with nobles and commoners alike. The aim was to move your counters from one end of the board to the other, with several people able to play at once. Gambling was common, with some people even gambling themselves into servitude.

What sports did they play at the ancient Greek Olympics?

Historical records date the first ancient Olympic games to 776 BCE. The games were originally held every four years in Olympia, in southwestern Greece, with competitors travelling from across the region's various states. The very first Olympics lasted just one day and had a single event – a sprint race.

No Biting, No Poking

Over time, more events were added. Between 396 BCE and the first century CE, the games spanned five days, including an opening and closing ceremony, a mass slaughter of one hundred oxen, a funeral ceremony in honour of a mythological hero and a day of prayer. There were lots of sports, but no team events: everyone competed as an individual. Events included three running distances on a wide track where 20 people could run side by side, wrestling, boxing, horse and chariot races, and the pentathlon – as well as a five-event competition comprising running, long jump, discus, javelin and wrestling. One of the toughest sports was the pankration – a primitive martial art that combined wrestling and boxing. Biting and poking out people's eyes were banned, but this largely rule-free sport could get ugly.

What Did They Win?

The ancient Olympic games were the inspiration for the modern Olympics, which began in 1896. Unlike today's victors, who receive a bronze, silver or gold medal, depending on their ranking, ancient Greek Olympians were all fighting to be the sole winner of each event – the *Olympionike*. Immediately after the event finished, the winner would be presented with a palm leaf by a judge. The crowd would applaud and throw flowers, and tie red skeins of wool around the hands and head of the victor. At the end of the whole contest an official prize ceremony took place in the Temple of Zeus. All the victors would be presented with a crown of olive branches, known as a *kotinos*.

Just as today's athletes often receive victory parades and lucrative endorsement deals on their return from the Olympics, the same was true for Greek *Olympionikes*, who were welcomed home as heroes by their city-states. Songs would be written in their honour, and if an athlete had won three events, he could commission a leading sculptor to create a portrait statue to commemorate his success.

Many athletes were sponsored by the state, which paid for such privileges, as their heroes' sporting achievements brought great prestige to their hometown.

FOR THE GODS

While the ancient games were, like today's games, an exhibition of strength and endurance, they also had an underlying religious significance for the Ancient Greeks. Iphitos, the king of the state where Olympia was situated, established the games to calm the anger of the gods and bring peace to the region. The games were organised in honour of Zeus, the king of the gods. And in some sense, peace was a big part of the event. The *Ekecheiria*, or 'Olympic truce', meant that city-states were obliged to stop fighting for a month to allow the 40,000 athletes, spectators and tradespeople from all over the country to travel safely to the event.

What was the earliest human rights charter?

In the British Museum resides an object called the Cyrus Cylinder. It dates from 539 BCE and is named for Cyrus the Great, the Persian ruler who founded the Achaemenid dynasty. This ancient artefact points to the first civilisation willing to document the rights of its citizens – paving the way for the freedoms we cherish today.

Cyrus Cylinder

The clay-baked cylinder was created, most likely on Cyrus's orders, after his peaceful invasion of the fabled city of Babylon. It's engraved in Babylonian script, and the writings tell the story of how Cyrus was chosen by Marduk, the city-god of Babylon, to take the city after Nabonidus, the last king of Babylon, had imposed work on all the city's people. The etchings talk about Cyrus's just and peaceful rule, his abolition of the forced labour practice, and how he returned deported people to the city, leading many to see it as an ancient precursor to the human rights charters that would follow.

Magna Carta

While it came many centuries after the Cyrus Cylinder, Magna Carta's principles underpin many of the laws, constitutions and charters that have followed it, including the Universal Declaration of Human Rights. Issued in 1215 by King John of England and revised throughout the 13th century, the document established important principles such as the fact that every man was subject to the rule of law and that every free man should have the right to justice and a fair trial.

How many secrets did Emperor Qin Shi Huang take to the grave?

At the northern foot of Lishan Mountain, in Shaanxi Province, is the burial site of China's first emperor, Qin Shi Huang. Discovered by well-digging farmers in 1974, the complex, believed to be the largest and most opulent of its kind, contains some 600 individual sites around a central grave mound.

Treasure Trove

Archaeologists and historians have theorised that workers from all corners of the empire worked tirelessly for nearly four decades to create this underground city, covering around 57 square kilometres. From the sites that have been excavated so far, it would appear the emperor, who died in 210 BCE, aged 39, was buried near to everything he would need in the afterlife, all made from terracotta and bronze. Two thousand terracotta soldiers, each unique in style and expression, are believed to be part of an 8,000-strong army. Archaeologists have also unearthed horses, chariots and weapons in the small part of the site they've managed to excavate. Pits believed to contain concubines and an elaborate palace have yet to be unearthed.

Mercury Rising

However, the secrets of the burial mound itself – which rises out of the flat landscape to a height of 51 metres – remain a mystery. The Chinese government is likely waiting until technology is able to ensure preservation of its contents – earlier excavations of the terracotta warriors led to their paint peeling off – and the safety of those who enter. Writings from the historian Sima Qian refer to mercury rivers inside the tomb, representing the Yangtze and the Yellow River, as well as traps that would fire arrows at any intruders.

How did the Romans turn death into daytime entertainment?

The Romans loved spectacle, and nowhere was this more apparent than in the public shows organised by their rulers. To remain in favour, Rome's emperors built vast venues, including the famous Colosseum and Circus Maximus, where animal hunts, public executions and even naval battles were staged – at the cost of many human lives.

Ludi Meridiani

Held in the empire's amphitheatres at midday, after the animal hunts *(venationes)* and before the gladiatorial battles, the *ludi meridiani* were considered a necessary form of social control. These public executions showed the people that the powers that be were running the show. Condemned criminals were the unlucky 'performers' in this spectacle, where they could face a number of horrifying ends. Those sentenced to death would be led into the arena partially clothed or completely naked, and often shackled to await their fate. This could come in the form of wild animals, an executioner *(confector)* or a fight to the death with other prisoners. In 'fatal charades', these unlucky souls were forced to re-enact mythical stories before they were killed.

Water Sports

The *naumachia*, or water shows, were extreme even for the Romans. While some *naumachia* took place in the Colosseum itself, flooded with water, many of these epic re-enactments were held in costly artificial basins built specially for the event. One impressive show put on by Augustus in 2 BCE saw 30 ships recreate the Battle of Salamis (480 BCE), with 3,000 men fighting to the death. It was set in a basin that measured approximately 136 metres by 357 metres – around the length of five football pitches – and filled with about 352,000 cubic metres of water. That's enough to fill over one hundred Olympic-sized swimming pools.

The men who played the parts of oarsmen and soldiers in these shows were usually prisoners of war or criminals. In another water show, staged by Julius Caesar in 46 BCE, 4,000 oarsmen rowed 2,000 soldiers into the fake battle, dressed in costumes as Egyptians and Tyrians. But while the battle was largely choreographed to reflect history, the fighting was real. Thousands died, either in combat or by drowning, to keep the Roman hordes entertained.

CHARIOTS OF FEAR

For those interested in fame and glory, chariot racing was the way to go. Gladiators, while popular with the crowds, had low social status, no different from prostitutes or actors. But charioteers were treated like heroes and famed throughout the Roman world. That's *if* you survived. Chariot racing was notoriously dangerous, with races seeing four charioteers speeding around the track while controlling two or four horses at once. The men would wrap the reins tightly around their wrists, so in the event of a collision they had to make a snap judgment whether to cut themselves free and risk being trampled by whatever was behind, or be dragged by their own horses into the fray. It's no surprise that many died pursuing their sport. The average age of death listed on charioteers' tombstones is just 22.

How did Mayan parents make sure their babies were at the height of fashion?

New parents today can spend a fortune kitting out their baby in adorable fashions and accessories – but contemporary culture pales in comparison to the lengths taken by ancient Mayan mums and dads to ensure their offspring were in vogue, from shaping their babies' heads to redirecting their gaze.

Heads Shaped Like Corn

Mayan ideas about beauty were heavily rooted in religious beliefs. The maize god, Yum Kaax, provided the inspiration for the sloped shape of their foreheads – as the elongated shape of an ear of corn narrows towards the top. Rather than a hereditary trait, this sloped head shape was created by artificial cranial deformation. Babies' head bones are relatively soft at birth to enable them to pass through the birth canal. The Mayan tradition took advantage of this, by binding a newborn's head between two wooden boards – one behind, and the other attached at an angle on top. The angle of the top board would be gradually reduced over several days to achieve the desired shape. Skeletal analysis of burial sites indicates that up to 90% of the population had endured this procedure as infants. Studies of skeletons found in Australia, the Bahamas and Germany show that the Mayans weren't the only ancient civilisation to meddle with their children's heads.

resemble the plant's individual kernels. As children grew into adulthood, they might have been wealthy enough to have a truly sparkling smile. This rite of passage was not a whitening procedure, as you might suspect, but rather holes drilled into the front of the teeth, inset with precious stones such as jade, obsidian or hematite. The stones were cemented using a plant-based adhesive so strong that many of them have been found in skulls by archaeologists today.

Eyes on the Prize

But for the truly dedicated parent, there were other lengths you could go to. Another highly desirable feature was slightly crossed eyes. To achieve this effect, parents would tie small soft balls or tiny stones to strands of their child's hair and position them in the centre of their face. Over time this could cause their gaze to become crossed.

Teething Problems

It wasn't just children who had to suffer for their beauty. Many Mayans would file down their teeth to a point or a T-shape. This is again thought to be a recognition of corn – their teeth would

EMBELLISHED BEAUTY

A long, Romanesque nose was considered the ideal complement to a Mayan's forehead. For those not blessed with the perfect beak by nature, there was the option of an artificial removable nose bridge to create the desired effect. Body piercings were commonplace, as was body painting. Permanent tattoos were less common, as the process was extremely painful and could cause infection and illness. Tattoos, therefore, were considered a sign of bravery.

What were the Greeks' most dangerous weapons?

The Greeks spent much of their time fighting each other, as ancient Greece was not a country but a number of separate states, including the main city-states of Athens, Sparta, Corinth, Megara and Argos. This means they had a lot of practice coming up with clever ways to defeat their enemies.

Spartan Soldiers

Some of these states were known for their formidable armies, none more so than Sparta. An old adage was that one Spartan soldier was worth several other Greek men. From the age of seven, all Spartan boys endured 13 years of training, known as the *agoge*, so they could fight for their city-state. Unlike other states' armies, which were drawn from men of various professions, Spartan men had one job for life, whether they liked it or not. Other roles in society were carried out by women, *helots* (or slaves) and the *perieoci* (neither slaves nor citizens, these were crafts- and tradespeople).

The Spartans were known for their spear, called a *dory*, which featured a bronze or iron spearhead at one end and a spike at the other. Known as the 'lizard killer', this spike came in handy for standing the spear upright, finishing off any fallen enemies as the army marched over their dying bodies, and, of course, for killing lizards. The soldiers also carried a *xiphos* – a short sword that could be used to reach through the gaps in enemy shield walls, unlike their foes' larger, unwieldy weapons.

Inventing Fear

Archimedes (ca 287–212 BCE) was born in the Greek colony of Syracuse. He devoted his life to philosophy, mathematics and inventing. When the Romans conquered Syracuse in 211 BCE, it was after a long and bitter siege in which Archimedes was instrumental. He was responsible for constructing the heaviest catapult ever built, which was capable of firing an 80-kilogram stone, as well as a mirror system that focused the sun's rays on enemy boats, setting them on fire. Archimedes was eventually killed by a Roman soldier, reportedly while in the middle of some absorbing calculations.

Fire and Brimstone

One dangerous weapon wrongly attributed to the Greeks, but actually invented by the Greek-speaking Byzantine citizens of the eastern Roman Empire in the seventh century CE, is 'Greek fire'. Thought to have been a petroleum-based mixture, Greek fire was launched from flame-throwing tubes on ships, igniting enemy vessels and soldiers.

RULING THE WAVES

Some Greek states, such as Athens, Corinth and Rhodes, commanded the Mediterranean Sea with enormous fleets of warships. The ships enabled them to build trading routes and transport soldiers to protect their colonies. The trireme was the most common of these ships and required 170 men to row it. The trireme's not-so-secret weapon was the sharp metal ram fixed to the front of it. This enabled the vessel to get close to an enemy ship, with the aim of crashing into it, causing severe damage and flooding.

Could you get a prenuptial agreement in ancient Egypt?

We tend to think of women's rights, in most cultures, as a relatively new thing. In ancient Egypt, however, women enjoyed a parity with men in most aspects of life. With divorce a possibility, the option of a premarital agreement or divorce contract provided women with power and security unmatched in other ancient cultures.

Contractual Obligations

At the Oriental Institute of the University of Chicago, United States, hangs a 2,480-year-old Egyptian annuity contract that promises the wife 1.2 pieces of silver and 36 bags of grain every year for the rest of her life, with or without her husband. Other existing legal documents from the time show a woman's personal possessions and finances recorded, so that her husband would know what to repay her in case of divorce. Women were also entitled to one-third of any of their husband's wealth that was acquired during their marriage.

Girl Power

Egyptian women often had to rely on men financially, as employment was one area where they did not enjoy parity with men. But, regardless of their marital status, they did have many legal rights. They could serve on juries and as witnesses in court, could sue and be sued, and could even own their own property, including slaves, lands and goods. Women would often make money by growing vegetables, making clothing and even renting out their own slaves, which they often clubbed together in consortiums to buy, making them more affordable.

ANCIENT HISTORY

Are you having a Roman holiday or is it still all Greek to you? Test yourself with this quick quiz to find out how much you've learned.

Questions

1. Which of the following sports was not featured at the ancient Olympics: chariot races, wrestling, kayaking?

2. The Incas dragged vast quantities of stone up the mountainside to build Machu Picchu – true or false?

3. Why did Roman emperors routinely poison themselves?

4. Is Magna Carta a cathedral, a sacred cart or a famous document?

5. How much water was in the basin in which Augustus's famous *naumachia* (water show) took place in 2 BCE – enough to fill a bucket, a bath or more than one hundred Olympic-sized swimming pools?

6. Which body parts did Mayans alter to honour their god of corn?

7. What were the terracotta warriors guarding?

8. Ancient Egyptian women were entitled to all their husband's wealth if they divorced – true or false?

9. *Ullamaliztli* and *patolli* were games played by which ancient civilisation?

10. Spartan men were automatically committed to what profession?

Turn to page 246 for the answers.

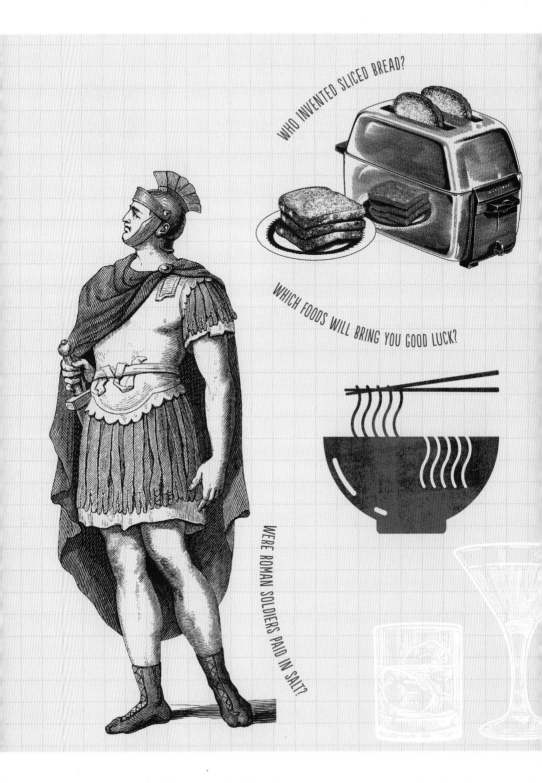

WHO INVENTED SLICED BREAD?

WHICH FOODS WILL BRING YOU GOOD LUCK?

WERE ROMAN SOLDIERS PAID IN SALT?

WHICH SOFT DRINK WAS MADE FROM 'THE LEFTOVERS OF LEFTOVERS'?

FOOD AND DRINK

DOES DRINKING ALCOHOL WARM YOU UP?

What's the world's spiciest food?

The Scoville scale measures the 'heat' or piquancy of chillies – the spiciest food on Earth. The capsaicin molecule binds to pain receptors in the mouth, causing the eyes to water, the nose to run and the skin to sweat, in an effort to rid the body of this toxin.

Spice Things Up

There are a few chillies that are universally agreed to be the hottest of the hot. These include the Bhut jolokia, or ghost pepper, used by the Indian military as a hand grenade ingredient; the Trinidad moruga scorpion – the name says it all – and the Carolina Reaper, which in 2013 became the Guinness World Record holder for hottest chilli. It averages 1.57 million Scoville Heat Units (SHU) on the scale, compared to the jalapeño's measly average of 2,500–8,000.

Scaling Up

Invented by pharmacist Wilbur Scoville (1865–1942), the Scoville Organoleptic Test, which determines where a chilli or chilli product sits on the Scoville scale, is not an exact science. The test involves a measured amount of capsaicin oil, extracted from a dried chilli pepper, gradually being added to sugar water in decreasing concentrations. When three of a panel of five trained tasters can no longer detect the chilli in the sample, then its SHU value is agreed. A bell pepper has a rating of zero SHU, while pure capsaicin has 16 million SHU.

The Scoville scale is highly subjective, depending as it does on the heat tolerance of five individuals. Also, as they taste multiple samples, there is a chance that they develop sensory fatigue, their mouth heat receptors

BHUT JOLOKIA

TRINIDAD MORUGA SCORPION

deadened to the strength of the weaker samples. More recently, high-performance liquid chromatography has been used instead to measure chilli strength and is considered more reliable. In this mass transfer process, a liquid containing the chilli sample is pressurised and then pumped through a column that separates the sample's various components, allowing researchers to measure the precise levels of capsaicin.

Branching Out

There are a couple of chemical compounds that feature higher than capsaicin on the Scoville scale. One is tinyatoxin, 331 times hotter than pure capsaicin, and the other, three times hotter than that, is resiniferatoxin. But you might have to settle for your mind being blown, rather than your mouth, because these are found only in two cactus-like plants native to Morocco and northern Nigeria.

SAUCY!

If you're brave enough to sample the hottest of the hot, perhaps you might like to try flavouring your favourite food with The Source hot sauce, a food additive that hits a staggering 7.1 million SHU. Or why not sample Blair's 16 Million Reserve – they made 999 bottles of these pure capsaicin crystals. And yes, the name refers to the number of SHU you'd experience if you tried it. But buyer beware! Capsaicin is a neurotoxin, and if consumed in large concentrations can cause seizures, heart attacks and even death.

JALAPEÑO

CAROLINA REAPER

Were Roman soldiers paid in salt?

The word *salarium* was introduced during Augustus's rule of the Roman Empire. It means a salary, everything a person needs to survive, and is derived from the Latin word for salt, *sal*, as this was essential to Roman life. But were hard-working Roman soldiers paid in salt instead of money?

Seasoned Tale

A *salarium* was given to soldiers, military officers and provincial governors and was to account for all the provisions they needed – clothing, weapons and food, including salt. Soldiers did not buy these items, but their cost was deducted from the *salarium*. Any cash left over, usually about 20%, was paid to the soldiers in coins for them to spend as they wished.

The Value of Salt

The first great Roman road, the Via Salaria, leads from Rome to the saline-rich Adriatic Sea. Salt was a precious commodity whose price was heavily controlled by the Roman Empire – it was increased to raise money for wars, then lowered to enable even the poorest people to afford this essential item. Carts filled with salt would travel along this eponymous road and all over the empire to serve all manner of purposes.

Salt was not only a food additive and preservative (see below), but also an antiseptic – it shares its Roman name in part with the goddess of health, Salus – and even a currency. Cato (95–46 BCE), a politician during the Roman Republic, made a provision of salt for his slaves of about 20 grams per day. It's unlikely a slave would have eaten this much salt, but it was probably traded with others. It's also believed some slaves were bought and sold for salt, probably the origin of the saying 'worth his salt'. Later biblical references to salt also emphasise its high value. In the book of Matthew, Jesus said, 'You are the salt of the earth,' to his disciples to illustrate how cherished they were.

Salty Language

'Salt', or 'sal', features as the root of many other Latin words and phrases – another sign of its importance in everyday life. 'Salad' is derived from 'salata', meaning salted things, because salt was used to season vegetables. Salt was also associated with fertility, possibly because fish, who live in the salty sea, were known to reproduce far more than land animals. The Romans used the word 'salax' to describe a man in love, literally referring to him as being in a salted state.

PASS THE SALT

Salt's preservative effects meant it held an important place in Roman kitchens. Salt was available in a number of different forms – there were golden-coloured salts from Cappadocia in central Turkey and even darker varieties that had absorbed flavours from dried wood. The Romans, even by our modern salty standards, consumed a lot of the stuff. In Apicius – a collection of Roman cookery recipes, believed to be compiled in the fourth or fifth century CE – one recipe suggests cooking a suckling pig in a pot with its own weight in salt.

What gives chewing gum its chew?

Most chewing gum is made from flavourings, colourings, preservatives, sweeteners and a synthetic gum base. It's the base, the insoluble part of the product, that gives gum its unique 'chew'. Each manufacturer uses a recipe of food-grade polymers, waxes and softeners to create their product's texture.

Poly-what Now?

A polymer is essentially a string of molecules, containing carbon and hydrogen. The ones in gum base are man-made, but they're identical in structure to polymers found in nature – and chewing gum's origins were actually natural. Humans have been chewing on something since time immemorial. Pliny the Elder (23–79 CE) once wrote about a plant-based derivative called *mastich*, enjoyed by the ancient Greeks, while Native Americans chewed spruce tree resin.

Protective Gum

In the mid-1850s, Thomas Adams, a New York inventor, was helping the exiled Mexican president, Antonio López de Santa Anna, to develop a form of rubber using chicle resin from the sapodilla tree. The resin acts as a

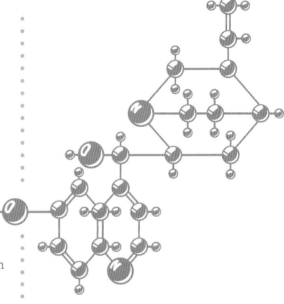

natural bandage, healing wounds in the tree's bark. Adams was unsuccessful, but soon realised he could use the resin as a base to develop a better form of chewing gum (prior to this, commercial chewing gum contained spruce resin or paraffin wax). The result was Chiclets – a candy-coated gum that's still available today. Synthetic polymers, which provided higher-quality and more consistent results, were widely used by the mid-1900s. It was just as well, because the rise in popularity for gum saw 25% of Mexico's sapodilla forests destroyed by 1930.

Who invented sliced bread?

Bread is consumed around the world in an array of portable forms, from French croissants and Polish bagels to Ethiopian *injera* and Indian *paratha*. It's the ultimate convenience food – but one American baker decided it wasn't quite convenient enough.

Slice of Success

In 1928 a bakery in Chillicothe, Missouri, United States, put the world's first commercially sliced loaves on sale. Otto Rohwedder was on a quest to bring the American people a more convenient form of their favourite starch. Although he'd taken great care to calculate housewives' optimum slice thickness – just under half an inch – bakers were still sceptical. They were worried that pre-sliced loaves would go stale more quickly – and they did. Rohwedder's solution was to insert a U-shaped pin into each end of the loaf to help it hold its shape and stay fresher. The 'power-driven, multi-blade' bread slicer was a success, and led to the English phrase to describe future great ideas: 'the best thing since sliced bread'.

Wartime Rations

During World War II, a wartime effort to conserve resources saw a ban on steel-produced bread-slicing machines in the United States. The ban was so unpopular, however, that it was lifted after just two months. In Britain, where white flour was usually imported from abroad, the government introduced a 'national wheatmeal loaf', which utilised the entire wheat grain, including the husks. It was an unpopular staple throughout the rationing years. Meanwhile, in Germany, the Nazi regime introduced *Kriegsbrot* – 'war bread' – made of rye, wheat and potato flour (occasionally mixed with sawdust) to keep people sated.

Which soft drink was made from 'the leftovers of leftovers'?

Fanta was born out of a World War II trading ban imposed on Germany. Max Keith took over Coca-Cola's German factory in 1933, and when war broke out six years later, the Allies' ban made shipments of cola syrup from the United States impossible. So Keith set his employees a task: to use their imaginations.

A Little Imagination

At the outbreak of World War II, Coca-Cola's German operations consisted of 43 bottling plants and 600 local distributors. Sales records were being set each year and Coca-Cola was making a name for itself across Europe. Not wanting to lose out on all those customers, Keith's challenge to his factory team was serious business. In German, the word for imagination is *fantasie*. And that's exactly what the German inventors of Fanta used to come up with this new concoction.

Lots of Leftovers

The fruit-flavoured Fanta varieties we know today, available in 188 markets around the world, are a far cry from the beverage that first bore the name, which was light in colour and resembled ginger ale. The ingredients

fanta
erfrischt
Brauselimonade mit Fruchtgeschmack

'The sugary drink was also used to flavour soups and stews.'

at their disposal were 'the leftovers of leftovers' from other food production facilities, and included whey, apple ibre from cider presses and beet sugars. In 1943 three million cases of Fanta were produced, although not all of these were being drunk. The sugary drink was also used to flavour soups, stews and other dishes during the years of sugar rationing in Germany. This tradition lives on in *Fantakuchen*, a popular German cake named in its honour.

HERE FROM EUROPE!

The first Fanta Orange bottles, using local citrus ingredients, were sold in Naples, Italy, in 1955. Fanta would go on to become Coca-Cola's second-largest-selling drinks brand after its namesake. But when it was first introduced to the US market in 1960, the advertising promoted its European heritage, declaring: 'French girls love Fanta too! (So will you!) It's the tangy treat from overseas.'

Drink Up

Fanta isn't the only soft drink with an unusual history. Here are a few others that might surprise you:

DOCTOR'S ORDERS Dr Pepper was created by a Texas pharmacist, who set out to create a soft drink that smelled like the soda fountain in the pharmacy where he worked. Once he'd hit upon the perfect recipe, he tested it on his boss, who approved and told him to start selling it in the store.

WHISKY AND SODA Brothers Barney and Ally Hartman, from Tennessee, United States, were fond of a whisky and soda, but in the 1930s they couldn't get the cola brand they liked in their hometown, so they came up with their own – the result was Mountain Dew.

CALMING EFFECT A drink called 'Bib-Label Lithiated Lemon-Lime Soda' was released in 1929. It contained lithium citrate – a relaxer that was widely used in the 1930s to treat mental illnesses. It continued to list this unusual ingredient until 1950, but changed its name to something a little catchier: 7 Up.

Who was the Pudding King?

When German monarch George I took the British throne in 1714, it was just a few months before Christmas. To make the celebrations extra special, he wanted his first festive season in power to include a traditional Christmas pudding. This earned him his nickname: the Pudding King.

A Ban on Christmas

This pudding proclamation was noteworthy, as only 67 years earlier Parliament abolished the feast of Christmas. This was under Lord Protector Oliver Cromwell, whose army of radicals had overthrown King Charles I. Cromwell and his Puritan supporters saw the festivities as sinful, believing God had not intended Christ's nativity to be celebrated with such waste and exuberance. The legislation remained in place until the restoration of the monarchy in 1660. During this period it was effectively illegal to sing carols, decorate with holly and ivy, and enjoy traditional festive treats. But by the 18th century, Christmas and its many trappings, including the pudding, were firmly back in favour.

Royally Sweet

George I is not the only royal associated with a delicious dessert. In Norway, a woman who taught the daughters of Prince Carl of Sweden and Norway dreamed up the Prinsesstårta (princess cake), a dome-shaped confection identified by its bright green icing. Battenberg cake – a marzipan-coated chequerboard of pink and yellow sponge – celebrated the marriage of English Princess Victoria to Germany's Prince Louis of Battenberg, while the Esterházy torta – meringue sponge layered with spiced buttercream – was named for Hungarian Prince Paul III Anton Esterházy de Galántha.

Do people prefer tea or coffee?

For some, choosing between tea and coffee is like choosing between your two best friends, but for many there's one clear winner, and that's often down to your country of residence. These beverages might not be the only way to start the day, but most countries tend to favour one or the other.

Trillions of Tea

Until the 18th century, coffee was mainly produced and enjoyed by Islamic nations, while tea was popular in East Asia, but the rise of free trade in the 1800s soon changed that. In terms of production, retail sales and the number of countries that favour it, coffee seems to dominate: 8.5 million metric tons of coffee is produced each year, which is double the amount of tea at 4.7 million metric tons. However, given that it only takes 2 grams of tea to make a cup, versus 10 grams of coffee, the world is actually producing coffee for a meager 850 billion cups a year, but enough tea for a whopping 2.35 trillion cups. That's 335 cups of tea a year for every single person – almost one a day.

Legendary Cuppa

According to popular legend, tea came to be in around 2700 BCE, when mythical ruler Shennong, the ancient Chinese 'Father of Agriculture', took a nap under a camellia tree with a pot of boiling water to drink. Dried leaves from the tree floated into the water and stewed, creating the first ever pot of tea.

Which foods will bring you good luck?

Fancy munching a fatty sausage, gobbling down a bowl of beans or slurping some soba noodles? Foodie superstitions from around the world are often focused on bringing prosperity and good fortune in the year ahead, so eat all three as you welcome in the New Year, and you might find it's your luckiest yet!

This Little Piggy...

A suckling pig is included in New Year's festivities in Spain, Cuba, Hungary and Portugal, among other countries. Folklore claims that pigs are animals of progress – they always move forwards when they're rooting around for food, and their high fat content symbolises wealth and prosperity. Germans eat a variety of pork-based sausages throughout the holiday season, and their Austrian neighbours decorate the New Year's dinner table with small pigs made from marzipan. But make sure you're not still eating Christmas turkey in the New Year – because these birds, as well as chickens, scratch backwards, it's thought they could bring you setbacks and struggles in the months ahead.

Something Fishy

If you're a fan of fish, you'll be pleased to hear that along with the many health benefits of eating seafood, there's also a lot of luck. Cod and other fish have been popular feast-time foods since the Middle Ages. Because they produce multiple eggs at a time, fish have long been considered a fertility symbol. In Japan you can pick up a *jubako*, a small food box filled with lucky foods for the New Year, which normally includes prawns, herring roe and sardines, to bring you a long life, fertility and bountiful crops.

BEAN THERE, DONE THAT

Beans in their seed-like form symbolise money, so many cultures cook up a bowl of legumes to welcome in the New Year in the hope that some cash will come their way. In Brazil, the New Year is seen in with lentil soup or lentils and rice, while in the southern United States black-eyed peas or cowpeas are eaten in a dish called Hoppin' John, alongside leafy greens, which represent the country's paper money.

Slurpy Snack

If you can control your New Year's hunger enough to eat a bowl of soba noodles delicately, you might just bag yourself a longer life. In Japan, China and some other Asian nations, if you can eat a bowl of the long buckwheat noodles at New Year without breaking or chewing them, then a long life is coming your way. But make sure you're done slurping by midnight, otherwise it's considered bad luck.

Chinese New Year

Symbolism features heavily in Chinese New Year – from the decorations to the gifts, but especially in terms of the food. Foods whose names sound similar to words such as 'gold', 'luck' or 'money' feature heavily. For example, tangerines and oranges are eaten in abundance – the word for 'gold' sounds like 'orange' and the word for 'luck' sounds like 'tangerine'. Oranges with leaves are considered even luckier, because the greenery symbolises longevity.

Does drinking alcohol warm you up?

There's nothing quite like a glass of something strong to help fight off the winter chill. But drinker, beware – while your skin may take on a rosy glow after a few alcoholic drinks, causing you to feel a rush of warmth, your core body temperature is actually dropping.

Perceived Warmth

Ethanol, the alcohol found in most booze, is a vasodilator. This means it has the effect of widening the blood vessels, in particular the capillaries just under the surface of your skin. More blood is able to pass through and the amount of blood under the skin's surface increases. This is why some people look flushed when they're drinking. You might feel warmer, too, because the increase in blood triggers heat-sensitive neurons in your skin that detect a rise in skin temperature.

This is fine if you're in a warm environment – the danger occurs when you go out in the cold. Normally, we feel the cold because our blood vessels have constricted and the blood has flowed away from our skin and into our internal organs to keep all the vital bits warm. With so much blood retained near the surface, rapidly cooling down, you might not feel the cold as much, but you'll be at a much higher risk of hypothermia.

Sweats and Shivers

Not only does alcohol lower your core body temperature, it also prevents your body's natural reflexes from kicking in to help warm you up. Normally, when your core temperature drops you'll start to shiver – a natural reflex, caused by your skeletal muscles shaking to create warmth. But a study by the Army Research Institute of Environmental Medicine showed that alcohol stops you from shivering, so it's even harder to get your temperature back up. A 2005 study also showed that another reflex, sweating, was wrongly triggered by the increase in blood flow to the skin, which only serves to speed up the drop in core body temperature.

Top Me Up

Drinking to excess might not warm you up, but you might experience a number of other interesting side effects.

DULL THE PAIN Alcohol can dull your perception of pain, due to the dampening-down effect on the signals your sensory neurons pass to the brain. However, this can lessen over time, requiring you to drink more to achieve the same effect.

RELEASE THOSE INHIBITIONS Alcohol can reduce inhibitory control in the cerebral cortex, the part of your brain that's associated with decision-making, social behaviour and information processing.

FEELING GOOD While alcohol is actually responsible for increasing the production of stress hormones, such as corticosterone and corticotropin, it also increases the release of dopamine – the chemical that makes you feel great – so you keep going back for more.

YOU SNOOZE, YOU LOSE Alcohol might make you sleepy, but if you've drunk a lot, the amount of slow-wave and REM sleep (i.e. good-quality sleep) you will have will be significantly reduced, as will your brain's ability to consolidate memories.

Where does the phrase 'Dutch courage' come from?

There's no escaping the strong association between downing a quick G&T and calming your nerves. The term 'Dutch courage' is believed to have originated during the Thirty Years' War (1618–48), when English soldiers fought alongside the Dutch and developed a fondness for their pre-battle tipple of choice: genever.

Genever Have Guessed!

King William III, often referred to as William of Orange, arrived in England in 1688 and wasted no time liberalising the gin-distilling laws, which led to a boom in gin production – and consumption! The subtle-flavoured beverage as we know it didn't come into being until the 19th century, so what used to pass for gin was a substandard version of Holland's popular genever, imports of which were heavily relied upon before William relaxed the laws. Genever, still the Netherlands' best-selling spirit, is based on a malt wine, distilled with juniper and large amounts of sugar, the resulting taste being more akin to sherry than to gin.

LONDON DRY GIN

With the invention of a new distilling apparatus, known as the continuous still, in 1827, English distilleries were able to produce a purer form of alcohol, which unlike its predecessor did not need to be disguised or sweetened. London Dry gin was born and English gins have come to dominate the world. The UK is the world's biggest exporter of gin.

FOOD AND DRINK

Stuffed full of tasty facts? Fill up your cup and settle in for a foodie quiz session.

Questions

1. Are you more or less at risk of hypothermia when you drink?

2. Which beverage has more cups produced every year – tea or coffee?

3. Victoria sponge cake is named after which famous monarch?

4. In Roman times a *salarium* was a spa resort where soldiers went to relax after fighting – true or false?

5. What popular confection did Thomas Adams develop from his experiments with chicle resin?

6. In which country was machine-sliced bread invented?

7. The Scoville scale measures the heat of what: the sun, chillies or the Sahara Desert?

8. Which popular soft drink was created by a Texas pharmacist?

9. Genever, also known as 'Dutch courage', was the precursor to which alcohol?

10. In many countries, which animal symbolises progress because it always moves forward when eating?

Turn to page 246 for the answers.

WHAT HAPPENED TO THE REAL WINNIE-THE-POOH?

WHAT DID VLADIMIR NABOKOV KEEP IN HIS CABINET?

CAN MUGGLES PLAY QUIDDITCH?

WHO INVENTED THE BRA CLASP?

LITERATURE

WHICH AUTHOR WAS ABLE TO SAY 'THE DOG ATE MY HOMEWORK'?

How long is Margaret Atwood's LongPen?

For internationally successful authors, the global book tour can take its toll. That's why Canadian literary legend Margaret Atwood envisioned a device enabling her to sign fans' books all around the world from the comfort of her own home. The LongPen, developed by robotics experts Syngrafii, was the result.

Technically

The prototype, built in 2005, was the first robot capable of reproducing biometrically perfect human handwriting. An author in one location chats to a fan at a book signing via video conferencing. Using a stylus pen, they write a message, sign their name on an electronic tablet and press 'send'. A robotic arm in the receiving station then reproduces the text on the fan's book – the pen is even sensitive to the speed and pressure used by the author. The LongPen comprises two 'pens': the stylus used by the author, and an ink pen that reproduces the writing. While the machine can 'reach' to the other side of the world, the pens themselves are regular-sized. The technology is now used in the finance, legal, government and healthcare sectors.

SCI-FI COMES TO LIFE

While Atwood is the first author to use a real-life robotic pen, she wasn't the first to envisage one being used in this way with video conferencing. In the 1911 science-fiction serial *Ralph 124C 41 +*, American writer, publisher and inventor Hugo Gernsback's titular character uses a 'Telephot' – a videophone – to talk to a woman in Switzerland while he's signing his autograph for her in New York.

What did Roald Dahl know about chocolate?

They say authors should write what they know. While Roald Dahl's stories were filled with unusual characters and fantastical scenarios, when it came to writing *Charlie and the Chocolate Factory* he was definitely harking back to his childhood, when he was a taster for one of the world's biggest chocolate factories.

Boarding and Gorging

Between 1930 and 1934, Dahl attended Repton, a boarding school in Derbyshire, where he and his classmates were guinea pigs for nearby Birmingham chocolatier Cadbury. Every now and then a cardboard box would arrive in the boarding house containing 12 different chocolate bars, as Dahl explains in his autobiographical book *Boy*. The box also included a piece of paper for the boys to note their score out of ten for each bar, and to make any comments. Dahl recalls that all the boys took their chocolate-testing responsibilities very seriously and that the experience opened his mind to the idea of inventing rooms in chocolate factories where new treats were dreamed up by men and women in white coats. Thirty-five years later, he would draw on those daydreams to create the world of Willy Wonka's extraordinary factory.

The Importance of Chocolate

Dahl loved chocolate so much that he dedicated an entire chapter to it in *The Roald Dahl Cookbook*, where he wrote his 'History of Chocolate', spanning the seven years (1930–37) when his favourite chocolate bars were released. He once told a group of schoolchildren that they shouldn't bother remembering the kings and queens, just these dates.

Can muggles play quidditch?

Even if you've never read J. K. Rowling's Harry Potter books or seen the film adaptations, you've still probably heard of quidditch, the broomstick-brandishing sport that forms an integral part of her wizarding world.

Not Just for Wizards

In Rowling's novels, it's a sport that's been played for nearly 1,000 years by the magical folk who, unbeknown to us, exist alongside us 'muggles', or regular non-magic humans. It's a seven-a-side aerial game that features four balls – a Quaffle, two Bludgers and a Golden Snitch. Each team has three goal hoops at each end of the arena, and the aim of the game is to score the most points by

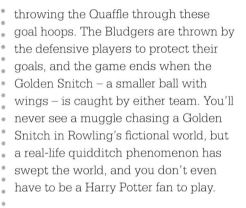

throwing the Quaffle through these goal hoops. The Bludgers are thrown by the defensive players to protect their goals, and the game ends when the Golden Snitch – a smaller ball with wings – is caught by either team. You'll never see a muggle chasing a Golden Snitch in Rowling's fictional world, but a real-life quidditch phenomenon has swept the world, and you don't even have to be a Harry Potter fan to play.

The Real-life Rules

To all intents and purposes, real-life quidditch is very similar to its magic counterpart. In this mixed-gender contact sport, two teams of seven are pitted against each other. According to the International Quidditch Association, players must wear coloured headbands to identify themselves as either the keeper, who guards the hoops at each end of the pitch where points are scored; the seeker, who must chase the 'snitch runner'; a chaser, who scores goals by throwing or kicking a volleyball through the hoops; or a beater, who must prevent the other team from scoring points by throwing dodge balls at them.

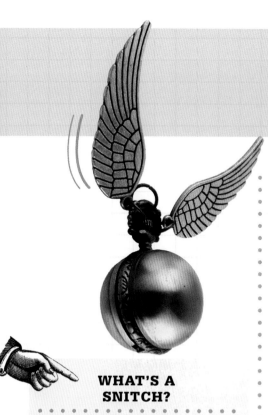

WHAT'S A SNITCH?

In Rowling's universe, the game only ends when the Snitch has been caught, so games can go on and on – three months is the record. According to the Pottermore website, the Golden Snitch replaced the Golden Snidget, an extremely rare, protected species of bird that was previously used in the game. In real-life quidditch, an independent athlete, who is also an official, takes the role of the Snitch runner. They must dress all in yellow and wear a tennis ball inside a sock dangling from their shorts. It is this ball that the seeker from each team is trying to get. Catching the Snitch scores the team 30 points and ends the period of play.

Making Magic Around The World

The real-life International Quidditch Association (IQA) serves some 20 national governing bodies across six continents. With teams in 26 countries, quidditch has become a popular sport for fans of Harry Potter and those who just love the game itself. Just like in the books, quidditch has its own World Cup, which has taken place every two years since 2012. The 2016 IQA World Cup was held in Frankfurt, Germany, and over 20 teams competed, including Slovenia, Brazil and South Korea; Australia won the tournament.

Why did the FBI have a file on Ernest Hemingway?

In 1983, after a Freedom of Information petition by an academic at the University of Colorado, United States, who was working on a biography, the FBI released a 122-page file on the American author and journalist Ernest Hemingway. The documents it contained spanned the years 1942 to 1974, despite the fact that Hemingway died in 1961.

Intelligent Operative

Between 1942 and 1944, Hemingway undertook intelligence work in Havana, Cuba, where he lived with his third wife, Martha. His activities were encouraged by Spruille Braden, the United States ambassador to Cuba, and he set up what he dubbed the 'crook factory' to keep tabs on the pro-Francisco Franco-Spaniards who had immigrated there and supported the German–Italian Axis. He was given $1,000 per month to pay his network of 26 informants.

Meanwhile, the FBI director, J. Edgar Hoover, ordered that Hemingway be put under surveillance. Hoover and others in the intelligence community believed Hemingway had ties to the Communist Party and that his intelligence information was not credible. The crook factory was dissolved in 1943, but the author continued to embark on submarine-hunting trips on his fishing boat for about two years. And the Hemingway file reveals that, even decades later, reports were filed about him and his phones were tapped.

The Toll of Surveillance

On 1 July 1961, at his home in Ketchum, Idaho, United States, Ernest Hemingway drew his favourite shotgun from his gun rack and, while his fourth wife, Mary, slept upstairs, ended his own life. His final year had been riddled with paranoia and depression. Friends of Hemingway have talked since about his belief that the FBI was keeping him under surveillance. He was also riddled with anxiety over his latest manuscript, a memoir about Paris, which would be published posthumously as *A Moveable Feast*. Seven months before his death, he was checked into the psychiatric wing of a Minnesota hospital, where he received electric shock treatments. During a release from the ward, he twice tried to kill himself, and while on a flight he tried to jump from the plane. All the while he believed the phones were bugged and the FBI was watching him.

One of the most recent reports in the file is dated 13 January 1961. Addressed to Hoover, it recounts how Hemingway was at that time a patient at the Mayo Clinc and that he was 'seriously ill, both physically and mentally'.

LIFE BEFORE LITERATURE

Despite dying at 61, Hemingway packed a lot into his life. Even before he'd published any of his novels, he'd already worked as a cub reporter for a Kansas City newspaper straight out of high school, and as a member of the volunteer ambulance unit in the Italian army during World War I. After the war, he worked as a reporter for both American and Canadian newspapers, covering events in Europe. In the 1920s, he worked as a correspondent in Paris, socialising with a group of international artists that included F. Scott Fitzgerald, Pablo Picasso and James Joyce.

'Between 1942 and 1944, Hemingway undertook intelligence work in Havana, Cuba.'

Who invented the bra clasp?

On 19 December 1871, Samuel L. Clemens was granted a patent for 'adjustable and detachable elastic straps for vests, pantaloons, or other garments requiring straps'. An illustration supplied with the application shows the inventor had devised an ingenious elasticated clasp, later to become a universal feature of bras. So who was this canny inventor?

(38.)

SAMUEL L. CLEMENS.

Improvement in Adjustable and Detachable Straps for Garments.

No. 119,322.   Patented Sep. 26, 1871.
No. 121,992.   Patented Dec. 19, 1871.

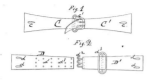

Witnesses:
Henry M. Miller
C. L. Evert.

Inventor
Saml. L. Clemens
per Alexander Mason
Attorneys

The Inventions of Mark Twain

Samuel L. Clemens was Mark Twain's given name. While his most famous works – *The Adventures of Tom Sawyer* and the *Adventures of Huckleberry Finn* – have become classics of American literature, his adjustable clasp has had a huge impact on the comfort and fit of women's lingerie for over 150 years. The patent also shows that Twain wanted the strap to be a flexible addition to clothing that could be attached and detached between different garments, to hold together any ill-fitting piece of clothing. 'When changing garments the strap may readily be detached from one and put

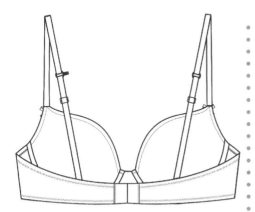

scrap books'. As a scrapbook enthusiast, Twain hoped to do away with the gluing element of the hobby with his self-pasting idea. The pages of the book would be entirely covered 'on one or both sides' with what Twain described as 'mucilage or other suitable adhesive substance'. It would only be necessary to moisten the part of the page you wanted to stick something to. The invention was a success and sold 25,000 copies.

on another,' he wrote. 'The advantages of such an adjustable and detachable elastic strap are so obvious that they need no explanation.'

Inventing Success

The device was a success and was used for shirts, underpants and women's corsets. Twain had hoped that his new invention would bring about the death of suspenders, which he found most uncomfortable. At the time, belts were largely decorative, so this elastic fastener provided people with another option for keeping their clothes in place. The 'bra clasp' was not Twain's only invention. He received two more patents – one, less successful, for a history trivia game that never went into production, and the second for an 'improvement in

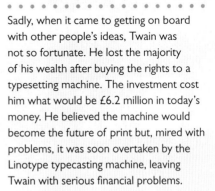

BETTING ON TYPE

Sadly, when it came to getting on board with other people's ideas, Twain was not so fortunate. He lost the majority of his wealth after buying the rights to a typesetting machine. The investment cost him what would be £6.2 million in today's money. He believed the machine would become the future of print but, mired with problems, it was soon overtaken by the Linotype typecasting machine, leaving Twain with serious financial problems.

What did Vladimir Nabokov keep in his cabinet?

Russian-American novelist Nabokov is internationally renowned for his famous novels, most notably the 1955 work *Lolita* – but he was also a distinguished entomologist. The pinnacle of this work is the 'Nabokov Genitalia Cabinet', containing hundreds of documents and cigar boxes filled with butterfly penises.

Wings and Things

Nabokov's passion for insects, especially butterflies, began from a young age, and developed into a serious study of lepidoptera when he enrolled at the Unversity of Cambridge. Twenty years later, after completing ten novels, he emmigrated to New York and soon began a six-year stint at Harvard, where he spent 14-hour days studying butterflies. At first his research led him to believe that a butterfly's key identifying feature was its wing pattern, but later he came to theorise that butterfly genitalia, only visible under a microscope, were more revealing of their evolutionary journey. As a result, he recorded and illustrated hundreds of these intricate anatomical structures and stored them methodically in a small wooden cabinet, now held in the Entomology Department of Harvard's Museum of Comparative Zoology.

Rewriting Science

During his lifetime, Nabokov's lepidopterology theories were not taken seriously – specifically, his belief that a particular genus of *Polyommatus*, the blues, had originated in Asia and travelled through Siberia and then south as far as Chile. Since his death in 1977, more attention has been paid to his work, and gene-sequencing technology has proved a number of his theories to be true. His professional work in the field ended after his time at Harvard, but he never stopped catching butterflies for his collection.

How did Dr. Seuss keep his publishers on their toes?

One in four American children receives a Dr. Seuss book as their first. The books have sold in the hundreds of millions and have been translated into 30 languages. His imaginative rhyming stories have captured preschool imaginations for decades, but one book almost featured a word not so suitable for bedtime reading.

Deceptive Contraceptive

To make sure his publishers were paying attention and actually reading his work, his manuscript for *Hop on Pop* contained the lines: 'When I read I am smart / I always cut whole words apart. / Con Stan Tin O Ple, Tim Buk Too / Con Tra Cep Tive, Kan Ga Roo.' Luckily, Bennett Cerf, the publisher, was reading intently and spotted the inappropriate word before it went to print. He no doubt read the author's work even more intently after that.

What's Up, Doc?

Dr. Seuss's real name was Theodor Seuss Geisel – Seuss was his mother's maiden name. He started using the moniker in college to conceal his identity. He'd been asked to step down as editor of the college magazine after being caught with a bottle of gin (this was during Prohibition). Instead of giving up as editor, he just used a pen name for all his bylines. Seuss should actually rhyme with 'voice', not 'goose', but eventually the pronunciation just stuck. The 'Dr.' he added as a nod to his father's hopes that he'd practice medicine. And while he was never a doctor of anything, he was granted an honorary doctorate in 1956.

What happened to the real Winnie-the-Pooh?

Winnie-the-Pooh, by A.A. Milne, was first published in 1926. With translations in 50 languages, including Czech, Afrikaans and Esperanto, sales of Pooh titles now exceed 50 million globally. But the honey-loving Pooh was inspired by a real-life black bear that most people know nothing about.

Bought Bear, $20

On 24 August 1914, Harry Colebourn, a captain in the Canadian Army, made a rather unusual note in his diary: 'Left Port Arthur, 7am, On train, bought bear, $20.' Colebourn, a veterinary surgeon, was part of the Canadian Army Veterinarian Corps on his way to the World War I battlefields. His mission: to look after the horses in the cavalry units. It comes as no surprise that this animal lover felt compelled to purchase the orphaned black bear cub, whose mother had been killed by a trapper, in White River, Ontario. He named her Winnipeg, shortened to 'Winnie', after his home town.

Winnie the Army Bear

At the start of the war, Captain Colebourn's regiment travelled to Europe, encamping at the Salisbury Plain training ground in Wiltshire, England. Winnie came along as a mascot and lived there with the soldiers for four months – she kept everyone entertained and was reportedly an excellent navigator. Unfortunately, this unlikely friendship was not to last. Knowing that his regiment would soon be sent to the front lines in France, on 9 December 1914 Colebourn borrowed a car and drove Winnie to the London Zoo. He asked the zoo to take care of her until he returned, but she soon settled in and became a star attraction for over 20 years.

A NEW FRIEND

Winnie's true star power, however, was still to emerge. Due to her friendly nature, she was trusted entirely by the zookeepers; they even let children go inside her enclosure, ride on her back and hand-feed her treats. As a result, she was beloved by children, none more so than a little boy named Christopher Robin, A. A. Milne's son. The father and son were frequent visitors to the zoo, and soon Christopher Robin had renamed his stuffed bear Winnie in honour of his new friend. While his father couldn't bring the real-life bear home, he combined her name with that of Christopher Robin's pet swan, 'Pooh', to create the name of a bear generations of children have enjoyed since.

When She Was Very Old

Winnipeg died of old age in May 1934, but her legacy lives on at London's Royal College of Surgeons' Hunterian Museum. Her skull was originally donated to a dental surgeon, who was the first to report on dental diseases in bears. He noted Winnie's loss of teeth, which he believed was caused by her old age and her food habits – it's believed Christopher Robin did in fact feed her honey and other treats. More recently, examinations have revealed that she suffered from chronic periodontitis – an inflammation or loss of connective tissues surrounding or supporting the teeth. Winnie's skull, along with those of other animals, has provided invaluable evidence to help zoo vets treat animals living in captivity.

QUESTION 75

Which author was able to say 'The dog ate my homework'?

Most children know the futility of the paltry excuse that their dog ate their homework, but, like most clichés, there's a little truth behind it. The celebrated author John Steinbeck knew that sinking feeling all too well, when he awoke one morning to discover his four-legged friend had transformed a first draft into confetti.

Too Poor for Paws

In 1933, Steinbeck was poor, living off his wife's pay cheque – it wasn't until 1939 that he would publish *The Grapes of Wrath*, widely considered to be his best novel, and a bestseller that once sold 10,000 copies per week. He wrote to his agent at the time, informing him he was so poor he couldn't afford a dog, or electricity. Steinbeck loved dogs and considered not having one akin to having the power shut off. His fortune soon turned, though, because a few years later he was well-off enough to have bought a setter named Toby.

A Nose for Good Writing

Toby made short work of destroying the manuscript that would later become *Of Mice and Men* in a frenzied night-time literary attack – two months' worth of writing gone in a flash. But while Steinbeck had to start from scratch, the book would go on to become a hugely successful novel, and he held his buddy's lack of appreciation in high regard, saying: 'I'm not sure Toby didn't know what he was doing when he ate the first draft. I have promoted Toby-dog to be lieutenant-colonel in charge of literature.'

Self-Destructive

The thought of intentionally destroying your own work would be more than most writers could bear. But for some, self-doubt, heartbreak and even mental health problems can lead them to wish for nothing more than for a dog to eat their latest manuscript. French novelist Gustave Flaubert, of *Madame Bovary* fame, anxiously buried a box of writings in his garden during the Franco-Prussian War. He died in 1880 and the box was never recovered. And Russian realist Nikolai Gogol, who published *Dead Souls* to great acclaim in 1842, burned the sequel after being persuaded by a fanatical priest that it was not good enough. He died ten days later. Some were luckier – their actions were not irreversible. English poet Dante Gabriel Rossetti condemned his poetry to the grave when he hid it in his wife's coffin, overcome by grief. Six years later he changed his mind and had her body exhumed so that he could finally publish some of his greatest work.

For others, their lifetime's self-doubt is overshadowed by posthumous success. Franz Kafka suffered from a crippling case of low self-confidence and only published a few pieces in his lifetime. He had asked his friend and literary executor, Max Brod, to destroy all his unfinished manuscripts upon his death, but his friend went against his wishes, leading to the publication of some of his most celebrated works.

How many languages did J. R. R. Tolkien invent?

J. R. R. Tolkien's famous novels – *The Hobbit* and *The Lord of the Rings*, published between 1937 and 1955 – have brought joy to generations of readers. Both stories are set in the imaginative world of Middle-earth. Its mythology is expansive and detailed, made apparent through Tolkien's use of language.

Scholarly Endeavours

John Ronald Reuel Tolkien's love for language was instilled early on by his mother, who taught him Latin, French and German at home. In a 1968 interview with the *Telegraph*, Tolkien said: 'When I was supposed to be studying Latin and Greek, I studied Welsh and English. When I was supposed to be concentrating on English, I took up Finnish.'

'It's possible that Tolkien invented over 20 new languages in his lifetime.'

He helped create the nonsense childhood languages Animalic and Nevbosh with friends, and later created his own called Naffarin, which was based on Latin and Spanish. But it was Tolkien's study of Welsh – he would go on to teach medieval Welsh at the University of Leeds for five years – and later Finnish that helped him to develop the mystical languages in *The Lord of the Rings*.

HOW TO SPEAK ELF

Rather than the languages being part of the stories, Tolkien saw the stories and world he created as a place for these languages, and the mythology surrounding them, to exist. In Ruth S. Noel's book *The Languages of Tolkien's Middle-earth*, she identifies 14 languages thought up by the author. But the two most developed Middle-earth languages are Quenya and Sindarin. Also known as High-Elven and Grey-Elven, these two Elvish languages have close ties to Finnish and Welsh, respectively, and their own historical language roots and dialects.

By the time the first two books in the *Lord of the Rings* trilogy were published in 1954, Tolkien had been developing these languages for 40 years. Quenya, which developed out of an earlier language called Qenya, is the Elvish version of Latin – it's a literary language used for poetry, song and magic. Sindarin, on the other hand, is the more commonly 'spoken' language, used by the Elves in his books to communicate. Tolkien's languages developed over time, even after the publication of the three *Lord of the Rings* novels. He made various changes to the Elvish texts in the second and revised editions.

Lost in Translation

None of Tolkien's languages were ever finished to the point where they could be used to fully communicate today, and some were only mentioned in the books but not spoken. There was also Dwarvish (known as Khuzdul), Entish and Black Speech, spoken by the servants of Sauron, including the Orcs. The latter is the language in which the famous 'One Ring to rule them all…' inscription is written. Middle-earth also features a number of 'Mannish' languages and dialects spoken by Men. Westron is the most commonly spoken language of Men, which is also spoken by Hobbits, and is 'translated' into English throughout the books for the reader. It's possible that, taking into consideration his Middle-earth work and earlier experimentation with linguistics, Tolkien invented over 20 new languages in his lifetime.

What is the longest book ever written?

Like the old adage 'How long is a piece of string?' the answer to this lengthy question is debatable. Some argue that a book's length should be measured in words; others say characters or even pages. But the Guinness World Record for the longest novel has stood for many years.

Time to Read

The title holder is *À la recherche du temps perdu*, or *In Search of Lost Time*, by Marcel Proust, which was published in a series of 13 volumes from 1913 to 1927. The novel contains an estimated 1.3 million words and 9,609,000 characters (including spaces). However, there are other claimants to the title. On word count alone, Madeleine and George de Scudéry's *Artamène ou le Grand Cyrus* (1649–1653), a ten-volume romantic epic containing an estimated 2.1 million words, is clearly a front-runner, while there are fan fiction stories online that run to well over 3 million words.

A Paper Trail

While the debate rages on, there's one manuscript that is a strong contender for longest physical book. A draft of Jack Kerouac's *On the Road*, now considered a 20th-century classic, was typed out by the author on a roll of paper that he'd taped together from 3.7-metre reams. The reason? So he could type continuously without being interrupted. The result was a 37-metre-long manuscript. In 2001, Jim Irsay, owner of the Indianapolis Colts, paid $2.43 million (around £1.9 million) for the scroll and loaned it to the Lilly Library at Indiana University in the United States.

LITERATURE

Literally stuffed full of facts? See how much of that bookish knowledge you've absorbed with this little quiz.

Questions

1. What did the LongPen device do? (And a bonus if you can name the first user!)

2. Which chocolate manufacturer sent taste tests to Roald Dahl's boarding school – Hershey's or Cadbury?

3. The Golden Snitch appears in which popular book series about a boy wizard?

4. Who invented the elastic clasp most famously used for bras?

5. Which language was not invented by J. R. R. Tolkien – Quenya, Sindarin or Klingon?

6. What did Ernest Hemingway do while he was in Cuba?

7. Vladimir Nabokov studied lepidoptera, otherwise known as which winged insect?

8. What word should 'Dr. Seuss' rhyme with – 'voice' or 'goose'?

9. How was Steinbeck's first draft for *Of Mice and Men* destroyed?

10. Winnie-the-Pooh was a real bear – true or false?

Turn to page 247 for the answers.

HOW DO YOU GET TO THE BERMUDA TRIANGLE?

WHO OWNS ANTARCTICA?

WHY WAS LAS VEGAS CALLED THE 'UP AND ATOM' CITY?

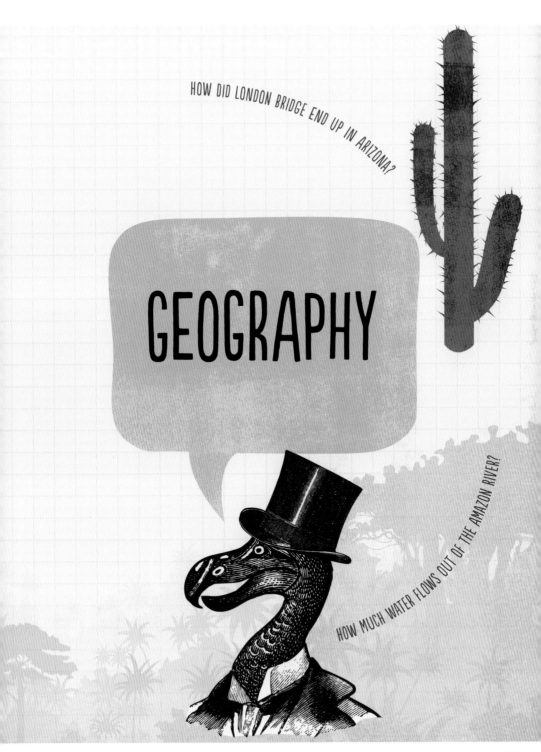

HOW DID LONDON BRIDGE END UP IN ARIZONA?

GEOGRAPHY

HOW MUCH WATER FLOWS OUT OF THE AMAZON RIVER?

How do you get to the Bermuda Triangle?

The Bermuda Triangle, or Devil's Triangle, covers roughly 1.3 millon square kilometres of the Atlantic Ocean between Bermuda, San Juan in Puerto Rico, and Miami, Florida, in the United States. The name was coined in a 1964 magazine article, after a number of mysterious disappearances and inexplicable activity made the region a hot topic for conspiracy theorists.

The Official Line

In a sense, there's no way to get to the Bermuda Triangle because technically it doesn't exist. The US Board on Geographic Names does not recognise the Bermuda Triangle as an official name, and no file is maintained on the area. In addition to this, there are no official maps that show the region's boundaries. If anyone should be cautious about the infamous Triangle, it's the US Navy and US Coast Guard, but both organisations claim that there are no supernatural forces at work. As yet, there is no hard evidence to prove that disappearances occur at a significantly higher rate in this part of the ocean than in any other well-traversed area. The Coast Guard's official line is: 'In a review of many aircraft and vessel losses in the area over the years, there has been nothing discovered that would indicate that casualties were the result of anything other than physical causes. No extraordinary factors have ever been identified.'

Going, Going, Gone!

Many mysterious disappearances over the years have led to the theories surrounding the Bermuda Triangle, but

arguably most occurred before modern advances in weather forecasting and communications. There was the 1920 disappearance of 11 crew members from aboard the *Carroll A. Deering* – the ship was later found off the coast of North Carolina, United States, with the crew nowhere to be found; then there were the five US Navy planes that took off from Fort Lauderdale, Florida, in 1945, never to be heard from or seen again; and then the 1948 vanishing of Captain Robert Lindquist and his plane off the Miami coast.

Triangular Theories

The region hosts most of the Atlantic's tropical storms, which would have been extremely dangerous for most ships and aircraft prior to modern forecasting technology. The Gulf Stream also makes the weather unpredictable, and the region's many islands mean waters are shallow and treacherous for large vessels. The bizarre disappearances of the crew from the *Carroll A. Deering* and the many other vessels and planes that have gone missing over the years have added fuel to the theorising fire. Some believe that extraterrestrials abduct humans from the region, while others believe a vortex is sucking these crew members into another dimension. There's also the theory that energy crystals from the lost city of Atlantis, which some believe sank here, are controlling the ships and planes above. But the more pragmatic types think most of these mysteries can be explained by science.

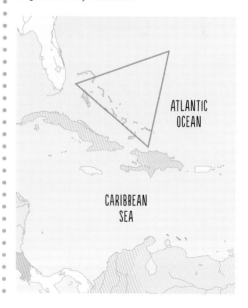

ATLANTIC OCEAN

CARIBBEAN SEA

How close have we got to the centre of the Earth?

The centre of the Earth is not a very hospitable place. At around 6,370 kilometres below the Earth's surface, the pressure is 3.6 million atmospheres – that's the same as having 47,700 elephants sitting on your head. It's no wonder we've literally barely scratched the surface when it comes to subterranean exploration.

Heating Up

The Earth is made up of a number of layers, which become increasingly hot the closer you get to the centre.

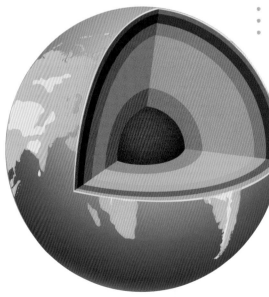

The outer shell, known as the crust, is about 50 kilometres thick, and for every kilometre you travel towards the Earth's centre, the temperature increases by 25°C. To put that depth into perspective, 1.6 kilometres is the average depth of the Grand Canyon or the bottom of Russia's Lake Baikal. Beneath the crust is the upper mantle, made up of partially molten rock, where temperatures are believed to range from 650°C. to 1,200°C. Under the mantle and the outer core lies the inner core, which scientists believe has a temperature of 5,700°C – roughly the same as the sun's photosphere.

Holey Moley!

These extreme temperatures mean that we've made few inroads into the Earth's crust. Drilling is the obvious method to get down there, but the extreme temperatures, combined with the friction created by the drill bit driving through the rock, mean that conventional drill-bit materials become unviable at a certain depth. The deepest artificial hole drilled by humans is the Kola Superdeep Borehole in Russia. Starting in 1970, engineers spent 19 years drilling and made it just 12.3 kilometres below the Earth's surface – not even a quarter of the way to the crust. And technically, we've never made it this far, just our machines. In second place is Mponeng Gold Mine, South Africa, where miners travel a distance of up to 3.9 kilometres below the surface. Eight of the deepest mines in the world are situated in South Africa.

JOURNEY TO THE BOTTOM OF THE OCEAN

The deepest artificial hole is only marginally closer to the centre of the Earth than the deepest part of the ocean. That's Challenger Deep at the bottom of the Mariana Trench in the Pacific. More people have been to the Moon than to this point on our own planet. In 2012, film producer James Cameron became the third person ever to reach the bottom of this near 11,000-metre-deep cavern, in a submarine called *Deepsea Challenger*. He spent three hours exploring the ocean bed and described it as 'quite a sterile, almost desert-like space'.

In 2015, one ongoing exploratory expedition attempted to use the Indian Ocean's depths to drill down to the Earth's mantle – a challenge attempted a few times but never achieved. They were aiming to target the Moho border, where the crust and mantle meet, to extract 'gabbros' – rocks created when slow-cooling magma is caught under the surface of the crust-mantle transition. Unfortunately, after nearly two months at sea, the researchers and crew of the JOIDES (Joint Oceanographic Institutions for Deep Sampling) Resolution returned to dry land after falling short of their planned 1,300-metre hole by 511 metres.

'At around 6,370 kilometres below the Earth's surface, the pressure is 3.6 million atmospheres. That's the same as having 47,700 elephants sitting on your head.'

Which point on Earth is closest to space?

The peak of Mount Everest might be the top of the tallest mountain on Earth, but there are a number of other places you could stand if you wanted to be closer to space. Ecuador's Mount Chimborazo is the closest.

Impressive Peaks

Everest holds its title because mountains are traditionally compared based on their height above sea level. So while Chimborazo rises 6.2 kilometres above sea level, Everest pulls in a whopping 8.8 kilometres. However, the inactive Andean volcano is the world's highest peak if you measure mountains from the centre of the Earth. On this basis, the peak of Chimborazo rises higher than any other mountain, at 6,400 kilometres – that's 2 kilometres farther from the centre of the Earth than Everest.

Shaping Up

So why the difference? It's all down to the shape of the planet. Earth is not a perfect sphere; it's slightly inflated around the middle – where equatorial countries are situated. Everest is located at 28 degrees north latitude, much closer to the North Pole, where the sphere flattens. Because the Earth's radius is about 20 kilometres wider at the equator, mountain peaks in countries like Ecuador and Kenya technically reach farther into space than their more earthly rivals, and Chimborazo is closest of all to the stars.

For those who like the idea of being on the top of the world but can't be fussed with all those weeks of training, hiking and acclimatising to scale Everest, reaching the top of Chimborazo is a much more achievable ambition – typically a one- or two-day hike after acclimatisation.

Why was Las Vegas called the 'Up and Atom' city?

Between 1951 and 1992, hundreds of nuclear tests, both underground and atmospheric, occurred in the Nevada Test Site, 105 kilometres north of Las Vegas, in the United States. During the 1950s and 1960s, mushroom clouds were visible from the casinos and hotels of the Strip, and postcards proudly proclaimed it the 'Up and Atom city.'

Atomically Correct

The US military had previously used Pacific Ocean sites to test nuclear weapons and their effect on American warships, but those sites were over 7,400 kilometres from the US mainland and required the efforts of 42,000 military personnel. As the pressures of the Cold War mounted, a closer location became essential. The 3,561-square-kilometre Nevada site was chosen based on its predictable weather, mountainous terrain, sparse population and limited public access. There was minimal concern about the danger to public health from radioactive fallout, despite the fact that Las Vegas fell inside the government's 200-kilometre radius safety guideline. A 1955 brochure assured residents that the radiation levels were 'only slightly more than normal radiation which you experience day in and day out wherever you may live'.

A Real Boomtown

Each of the 928 nuclear tests was strategically planned to help determine how the bombs would work in different weapons. Other experiments were more concerned with the effect nuclear war might have on American lives. Residential houses and other infrastructure buildings were built in the test area and the effects of the blasts were carefully studied. Known as Survival Town, these fake homes came complete with mannequin families and everyday household items – even tinned food.

How much water flows out of the Amazon River?

The Amazon River might dispute its title for world's longest river with the Nile, but there's no denying its position when it comes to its water flow. At a staggering 219,000 cubic metres per second, the average discharge from this mighty South American behemoth is shoulders above the competition.

Wild River

To put this in perspective, every second of every day the volume of nearly 90 Olympic-sized swimming pools is gushing out of the Amazon's mouth – an estimated one-sixth of the world's rivers' discharge. And this is an impressive mouth. Where the river meets the Atlantic Ocean in eastern Brazil, its delta is 322 kilometres wide and features the world's largest freshwater island, Marajó, which is roughly the size of Switzerland.

Rainy Days

Where does all that water come from? A network of approximately 1,100 tributaries, which carry water a distance of over 6,600 kilometres, span an area of around 7 million square kilometres. The country of India covers only 3.4 million square kilometres. The vast quantities of water are thanks to the torrential rainfall the huge Amazon basin receives – between 150 and 300 centimetres per year, depending on the location. The rain is thanks in part to eastern trade winds blowing in off the Atlantic and also the vegetation that makes up the Amazon's biome. Water is soaked up through the soil by plants, evaporates, and falls as rain back into the basin. And as the weather changes, so does the river. Parts that can measure 2 or 3 kilometres across when it's dry can become 50-kilometre chasms in the wet season, with river speeds of up to 7 kilometres per hour.

West Meets East

The mighty river starts high up in the Peruvian Andes and makes its way east. But the source is a mere 193 kilometres from where the river used to end. Millions of years ago, the river emptied into the Pacific instead, but the collision of the South American and Nazca tectonic plates brought about the creation of the Andes mountain range about 65 million years ago. Eventually this blocked the flow of the river, creating freshwater lakes and gradually reversing the river's flow. It's estimated that the river reached the Atlantic Ocean about 10 million years ago.

SOMETHING FISHY

With all that water, it's no surprise that the Amazon is home to an astonishing array of life. It's estimated that over 2,500 different fish species are living in the river – more than the entire Atlantic Ocean – with some experts believing the number could be significantly higher. The biodiversity of the region has led to catfish weighing over 90 kilos, 5-metre-long arapaima, and the parasitic candiru – a tiny fish that has been known to swim up the urethra of people who urinate in the river. And if that's not terrifying enough, bull sharks, which have the ability to adapt from their usual saltwater habitat to that of the river, have been found as far as 4,000 kilometres upstream from the sea.

Who owns Antarctica?

On 1 December 1959, 12 countries entered into the Antarctic Treaty, stating that all parties '[recognise] that it is in the interest of all mankind that Antarctica shall continue forever to be used exclusively for peaceful purposes and shall not become the scene or object of international discord.'

Icy Claims

Of the 12 signatory countries, all of which had had scientists active in Antarctica between 1957 and 1958, seven – Argentina, Australia, Chile, France, New Zealand, Norway and the United Kingdom – had existing territorial claims to parts of the continent. While the treaty states that nobody holds ownership of any land on Antarctica, it technically protects those claims and prohibits further claims from being made. One large segment of Antarctica was not claimed at the time of the treaty and remains the largest segment of unclaimed land on Earth.

In Agreement

Since the original 12 nations signed the treaty, 41 other countries have signed up to the same agreement. Among other things, they are committed to carrying out their work peacefully and cooperatively, with no military presence, and to sharing any scientific observations and results made from Antarctica with the other nations. No nuclear explosions or mining are permitted. The future importance of Antarctica is plain to see: it's believed to hold significant oil reserves, and has 70% of the world's freshwater supply.

How high up can humans live?

The peak elevation for permanent human residence is widely considered to be 5,200 metres. Above this altitude, life would be a struggle. Altitude sickness, which can affect people from 2,500 metres, can cause oxygen deficiency (which damages cells) and a deadly build-up of fluid in the lungs and brain.

Going for Gold

The world's highest city lies in the Peruvian Andes, on the side of Mount Ananea. With a population of some 50,000, La Rinconada sits beside a giant glacier, at a height of 5,100 metres. Despite the fact that the city lacks amenities and temperatures are sub-zero most of the year, the population has soared in recent years due to a gold-mining operation located several days' walk away along a precarious road. The mines are largely unregulated and run illegally, and miners are paid by an ancient system known as *cachorreo*: they work unpaid for 30 days but can keep any gold they find on the last day of the month. Every day they face perilous working conditions and high levels of mercury and cyanide.

Great Adaptations

Research has shown that communities that live at such high altitudes for significant periods, such as the Himalayan Sherpas, develop genetic adaptations to cope with the extreme conditions, such as compactly built bodies with adapted hearts and lungs. But it's unlikely the residents of La Rinconada would want to live much higher up, even if their bodies could handle it, because it would be impossible to grow crops or keep livestock.

How did London Bridge end up in Arizona?

Lake Havasu City lies on the Colorado River in Arizona, United States, and is connected to a small island in the lake itself, created by one of many dams along the river, by a rather unusual-looking landmark – London Bridge, shipped all the way from England in 1968.

Bridging the Gap

The city is home to over 50,000 residents, but that wasn't always the case. In the 1960s its population was less than 4,000 and it was considered an arid backwater, unworthy of a visit. The city's founder – Missouri-born industrialist Robert McCulloch – had purchased thousands of acres of land beside the lake in the hope of creating a tourist mecca, but was having trouble bringing in the crowds. When he heard that the City of London was selling a 130-year-old bridge, he knew it would be the perfect draw for his fledgling community.

Selling Up

The London Bridge that found itself the object of McCulloch's affections in the 1960s was not the medieval London Bridge commissioned by King Henry II in 1176. That bridge was the first permanent stone crossing to join the north and south banks of the river Thames. The granite bridge that ended up in the Arizona desert was the one that replaced it some 600 years later, in 1831. Designed by John Rennie and

completed by his son, it was over 300 metres long and survived London's Blitz during World War II. However, the toll of 20th-century traffic was weighing on it, literally, and London Bridge was falling down at a rate of 2½ centimetres every eight years. The city decided to replace it with a wider, more car-friendly crossing, and it would have ended up as scrap if one city councillor hadn't come up with the ingenious idea of selling it.

'Designed by John Rennie and completed by his son, London Bridge was over 300 metres long and survived London's Blitz during World War II.'

A BRIDGE TO NOWHERE

Ivan Luckin, the optimistic councillor, pitched the bridge as an historic heirloom. And while many thought buying a bridge from England was a ridiculous notion, it was exactly what McCulloch was looking for. A price of $2.46 million (£1.9 million) was agreed, and then began the mammoth task of dismantling, transporting and reassembling the giant antique over 8,000 kilometres away. The bridge wasn't long enough to cut across the lake itself, but this didn't faze McCulloch – it was assembled over land, connecting the main shoreline with a peninsula. When the work was nearly completed, a channel was cut through the joining piece of land to create an island. It took three years and $7 million (around £5.5 million) to complete the project, but it had the desired effect – the population boomed, and just three years after completion some 10,000 people were calling Lake Havasu City their home.

Which sea has no coastline?

QUESTION 16 QUESTION

The Sargasso Sea is situated in the North Atlantic Ocean, which makes it the only sea with no land boundary. It's measured at approximately 1,600 kilometres long by 5,000 kilometres wide – roughly two-thirds of the ocean that contains it.

Coasting Along

Typically, seas are found on the fringes of the oceans, and are partially enclosed by land, but the Sargasso Sea is one of a kind. Rather than being defined by land boundaries, its perimeter is determined by ocean currents. Its northern, eastern, southern and western extremities are decided by the North Atlantic Current, the Canary Current, the North Atlantic Equatorial Current and the Gulf Stream, respectively. While these strong currents contain the sea, the currents within it are fairly stationary, and the temperatures significantly warmer than the surrounding ocean.

Special Seaweed

The sea is named for the large mats of dense sargassum seaweed that live on its surface. This free-floating alga is different from other types of seaweed in that it reproduces on the surface, rather than the ocean floor. It provides a diverse home for a wide variety of species, as well as a feeding ground for migratory animals that pass through it, including humpback whales and bluefin tuna. Christopher Columbus is thought to have mistaken the floating patches of sargassum as an indication that he was close to land, when he was still many hundreds of kilometres from the shores of the Americas.

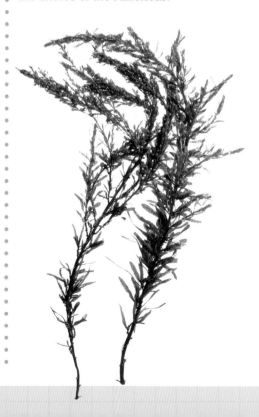

GEOGRAPHY

Find out how worldly you really are with this quick round-the-world quiz.

Questions

1. Where is the largest segment of unclaimed land on Earth – the Arctic or Antarctica?

2. The perimeter of the Sargasso Sea is defined by ocean currents – true or false?

3. In which country is the world's highest city – Peru, Poland or Portugal?

4. Which film director, known for blockbusters like *Titanic* and *Avatar*, has been to the bottom of the Mariana Trench?

5. The world's largest freshwater island, Marajó, is situated in the mouth of which river – the Nile, the Thames or the Amazon?

6. Mount Everest is the tallest mountain on Earth, and Mount Chimborazo is the highest if you measure from the centre of the Earth out. Which one takes longer to climb?

7. Which American state bought London Bridge in 1968?

8. Which city, situated near a nuclear test site, was known as the 'Up and Atom' city?

9. Disappearing planes, ships and crew members are all associated with which tropical region?

10. The Amazon River used to flow in the other direction – true or false?

Turn to page 247 for the answers.

WHY ARE TENNIS BALLS YELLOW AND FUZZY?

WHAT DO BIRDS HAVE TO DO WITH GOLF?

WHY IS THE TOUR DE FRANCE'S YELLOW JERSEY YELLOW?

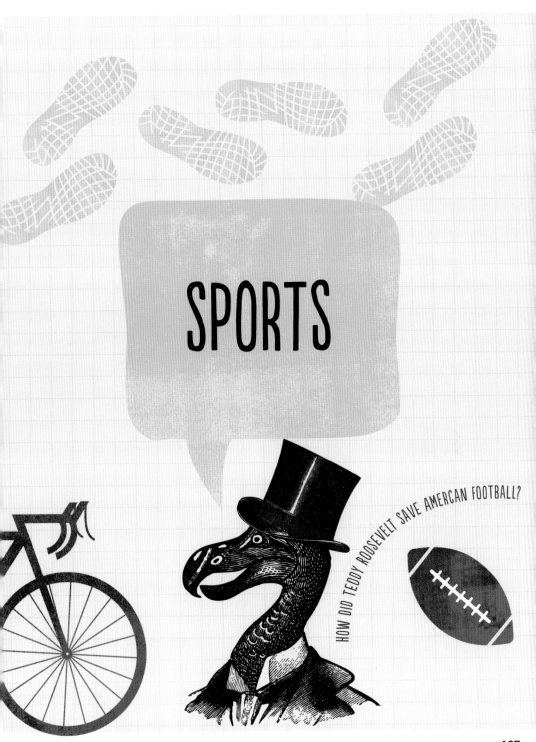

SPORTS

HOW DID TEDDY ROOSEVELT SAVE AMERCAN FOOTBALL?

Are we getting faster?

In 1935, Jesse Owens's fastest 100-metre time was 10.3 seconds. In 2009, Usain Bolt ran that distance in 9.58 seconds. It would be natural to assume our species is getting progressively faster. But the increasing speeds have more to do with technology and a wider gene pool being involved in high-profile sports.

Tech on the Track

When Jesse Owens stepped into the arena in the 1930s, he had a trowel to dig holes in the track – homemade starting blocks. The starting blocks aren't the only thing that's different today. Sports science and nutritional research have helped contemporary athletes to maximise their training regime, from high-carbohydrate gels and isotonic drinks that provide the right balance of fluid and fuel for long-distance runners, to ultra-lightweight running shoes with carbon soles and oxygen tents for a good night's sleep before a big race.

When it comes to sprinting, track technology has changed dramatically – Owens ran on cinders (pieces of rocks and burned wood), rather than the specially fabricated surface used today for running tracks. Where older tracks combine traction and shock absorption in a top layer of rubber, the latest technology separates these functions into two rubber layers: a cushioned backing to absorb the shock and a solid

top layer to reduce slip and optimise traction and durability. This provides a more flexible surface, reducing the amount of time the athletes' feet are in contact with the ground. Even the spikes on runners' shoes, which were once made from steel and then ceramics, are today made from newly developed lightweight carbon nanotubes – these minimise the amount of energy absorbed by the track on impact. Analysis of Owens's joints has shown that, were he to have had the same advantages as Bolt, he would have finished only one stride behind the Jamaican legend.

THE GENE POOL

Something that is changing, however, is the gene pool of athletes competing in international competitions. As sports and sports science are introduced to new populations, and as sports have become monetised, the human bodies with the optimum physiologies to excel in each sport have come to the fore. For example, in the early 1900s, long-distance runners were largely all of the same medium build, and similar to competitors in other sports. Then Kenyan runners came on the scene in the 1980s. The country, with a population of 41 million, dominates the long-distance racing scene, along with Ethiopians and Tanzanians. The majority of the Kenyan champions come from an ethnic minority that makes up just 0.06% of the population, the Kalenjin. The group is known for having less body mass in relation to their height, longer legs and a shorter torso, and slender limbs. Some studies have also found a higher number of oxygen-carrying red blood cells in this group. All are characteristics advantageous for long-distance running.

What's the farthest someone's travelled while surfing a wave?

In 2016, to raise money for the Human Variome Project, Australian surfers James Cotton, Roger Gamble and Zig Van Sluys rode the Bono tidal bore in Kampar River, Sumatra, Indonesia, for over 17 kilometres – and broke the world record for the longest surfing ride on a river bore.

Ebb and Flow

This record was made possible by the natural tidal bore phenomenon. There are approximately 60 similar bores found around the world, caused by rising water from the world's oceans washing inland up a gradually narrowing river. On certain days of the year, when the incoming tide is highest, a vast quantity of water is forced up these estuaries, dramatically changing the volume of water in the river. The speed of the surging 'top layer' of water creates a full-blown tidal wave. The Sumatran bore is known to the locals as 'Seven Ghosts'.

Record-Breaking Surf

However, this natural wave surf pales in comparison to the 66.5 kilometres that Gary Saavedra from Panama spent surfing behind a wave-creating boat in 2011. That's about the same distance as from Washington, DC, to Baltimore. He holds the Guinness World Record for the longest distance surfing a wave as well as the longest time spent surfing a wave in open water: 3 hours, 55 minutes, 2 seconds. Incidentally, the farthest a dog has ever surfed is 107.2 metres. The record was set by Abbie Girl, an Australian Kelpie, in San Diego, California, United States.

What do birds have to do with golf?

Golf began life as a Scottish pastime, but its curious avian terminology is all thanks to its American history. The term 'birdie' (a score of one stroke under par, par being the score standard for each hole on the course) is believed to have originated at the Country Club in Atlantic City, New Jersey, United States.

Brilliant Birdie

'Bird' was an American slang term meaning excellent or outstanding. In 1903, Abner Smith teed off from the Country Club's 12th hole. His second shot from the fairway landed a few inches from the hole, and his third shot was an easy putt, putting him one under par. Someone in his group shouted, 'That was a bird of a shot!' News of the 'birdie' spread, and within ten years players around the world were also using the term.

Rare Breed

An 'eagle' and an 'albatross' were natural extensions of the birdie, the former meaning two under par and the latter three under par – the rarer bird for the more impressive play. But while 'eagle' was introduced by American players, 'albatross' was down to the Brits. The first albatross to feature in a news report was in 1931 when a South African player named E. E. Wooler scored a hole-in-one on the par-four 18th hole of the Durban Country Club. British journalists reported this as an albatross. Many American players, however, still refer to three under par as a 'double eagle'.

What is the world's most dangerous sport?

Participants in BASE jumping leap from low altitudes, such as from the top of a high building, before opening a parachute. By August of 2016 there had already been 31 deaths that year, and it's estimated that one out of every 2,317 jumps ends with a fatality – more than any other sport by a long shot.

Not So Safe

Most people will never go BASE jumping, but the more popular triathlon's combination of running, cycling and swimming makes it extremely dangerous. One out of every 68,515 competitors is expected to die from competing. This was based on analysis of nearly 960,000 participants, where 14 had died as a result (13 from the swimming stage of the event). Another study by the University of California compared skiing and snowboarding and found that 49% of injured snowboarders were beginners compared to 18% of skiers, making it one of the most dangerous sports for novices. The risk of sustaining a head injury from skiing, however, is just as likely as with cycling and American football.

NOTHING TO CHEER ABOUT

Statistics published in the US *Journal of Pediatrics* in 2013 found that, in women, 66% of sports-caused permanent disabilities occur as a result of competitive cheerleading. Out of 26,786 high school and college cheerleading injuries in one year, 110 resulted in permanent brain injury, paralysis or death. Disproportionately, it is the bases – the people at the bottom who support those doing the aerial acrobatics above – who end up with the life-changing injuries.

Why are tennis balls yellow and fuzzy?

Historically, tennis balls were black or white, depending on the colour of the court they were used on, but in 1972 the International Tennis Federation introduced fluorescent yellow balls to the game, as research had shown that yellow was most visible for television audiences. Wimbledon, however, stuck with the white ball until 1986.

Make a Fuzz

The fuzzy felt coating on a tennis ball is one of its other distinctive characteristics. While it may make the balls seem less intimidating, it's true purpose is all to do with aerodynamics. The ball's surface affects its speed as it flies through the air – the fuzzier the ball, the slower its speed. That's why professional tennis players often inspect multiple balls before deciding on one to serve with – they're looking for a ball where a lot of the fuzz is lying flat against the ball's surface, for maximum speed and spin.

Serving Sheep Stomach

Tennis was developed from a popular European game, played since the 12th century, known as 'real tennis'. While today's tennis balls are made from two pieces of rubber sheet, sealed and pressurised and then coated in a felt-like cloth, real tennis balls were made from all manner of things including sheep stomach, human hair, sand, putty and cork.

What do a waffle iron and trainers have in common?

Blue Ribbon Sports was founded in 1964. Its owners were Bill Bowerman, a track and field coach at the University of Oregon, United States, and former UO alumnus Phil Knight, and they distributed trainers for a Japanese manufacturer. In 1971, Bowerman had an idea for an innovative shoe – and Blue Ribbon Sports became Nike Inc.

Waffly Workout

Bowerman's main job was as a coach, and the times they were a changin'. Orgeon's Hayward Field – the athletics track where he worked – was upgrading its facilities, including a new artificial surface. Bowerman knew the athletes needed a running shoe with a sole that would grip well on grass and bark dust. Running shoes hadn't changed much in over 50 years; he needed an innovative solution. The conundrum was on his mind one morning over breakfast when his wife was making waffles. The waffle iron's pattern proved to be his inspiration.

Bowerman had a home laboratory, and according to his wife Barbara, 'He got up from the table and went tearing into his lab and got two cans of whatever it is you pour together to make the urethane, and poured them into the waffle iron.' The rubber mould created from the waffle iron would be used as the inspiration for Nike's first shoe: the Waffle Trainer. The raised nubs created by the waffle-inspired mould would become Bowerman's first patent – he ended up with a total of eight. His designs would go on to inspire other classic Nike shoes, including the Nike Cortez and the Moon Shoe.

THE NIKE 'SWOOSH'

In 1971, the year Blue Ribbon became Nike, a young graphic design student named Carolyn Davidson was paid $35 by Phil Knight to come up with a logo for the new shoe brand. She was working for him on a $2-an-hour rate and spent just 17.5 hours coming up with the design. Davidson's Nike 'swoosh' has become one of the most recognised logos in the world. She later received a significant number of shares from Nike, worth hundreds of thousands of dollars – not bad for a few days' work.

Unearthed Treasures

So what became of the waffle iron used to make those first prototype soles? It was thrown into the scrap heap in the Bowermans' back garden. The rubbish truck would not come to their house, so the family would bury their rubbish in a pit out in the garden, and the destroyed waffle iron went in that pit too. But in 2011, when one of Bowerman's sons was looking to remodel the family's shop, he excavated the yard to pour a new foundation. That was when the 15-centimetre, 1930s waffle iron, which had been a wedding gift to the Bowermans, emerged from the soil. The family contacted Nike and traded the iron for sporting equipment for a local athletics programme.

'The rubber mould created from the waffle iron would be used as the inspiration for Nike's first shoe: the Waffle Trainer.'

Who was responsible for the first basketball 'swish'?

A 'swish' in basketball is when a player makes a shot through the hoop where the ball doesn't touch the rim or the backboard – it simply passes right through the net, making that swishing sound that players and fans love to hear. But there was a time when basketballs didn't swish.

The Sound of Success

Basketball was invented in 1891 by Dr James Naismith. But there was an obvious reason it was called 'basket' ball. The original game was played with two peach baskets fixed to posts or the balconies of running tracks in indoor sports facilities. Nets began to make an appearance in 1893, but even then they were still metal and closed-ended, so players had to fish out the ball each time to continue play – no swishes there. Over 20 years after the game was first played, in 1912, open-ended fabric nets became approved for use in high school and college games.

The Swish in Writing

The first real-life recorded swish (swishes were written about in fiction as early as 1913) is believed to belong to a Brooklyn player named George Edelstein. A writer in the *New York Tribune* observed the Bushwick High School player had only four shots where he failed to 'send the ball swishing through the basket for a point'. And so the swish was born.

Where was table tennis invented?

Table tennis is an international sport of agility, speed and skill, but its origins lie in the after-dinner amusements of British soldiers stationed abroad in the late 1800s. Then it wasn't known as table tennis, or even ping-pong, but by the whimsical name 'whiff-whaff'.

After-Dinner Dalliance

There's a dispute about the precise birthplace of table tennis – the military mess halls of India, Malaysia or Asia Minor are all candidates. In an attempt to bring the popularity of tennis to an indoor setting, soldiers and the English gentry would hit a wine cork back and forth across a table using cigar box lids. The net was a wall of stacked books. Thus, the game could be played anywhere, with anything and by anyone. Around the world, many languages refer to the sport literally as table tennis. In French it's *tennis de table*, in German *Tischtennis*, in Dutch *tafeltennis,* and in Norweigan *bordtennis*. But in Chinese, the phonetic pronunciation *Pingpang qiú* is more similar to 'ping-pong'.

Ping-Pong Takes Off

In 1901, the Jacques games company trademarked the name 'Ping Pong' after the sound the new celluloid ball made when it hit the table and the rackets (also known as paddles and bats), which had a solid wooden frame and handle and were covered with stretched vellum. Soon, standardised rules were introduced and the two rival associations – the Table Tennis Association and the Ping Pong Association – united in 1903 to form one governing body. Later introductions of sponge-coated rackets with rubber top layers transformed table tennis into the fast-paced sport we know today.

How did Teddy Roosevelt save American football?

As the 20th century got underway, American football was almost as popular as baseball in the Unted States, with tens of thousands attending college games. But it was a treacherous sport that had left dozens of players dead – until President Theodore Roosevelt stepped in and transformed the brutal game into the phenomenon we know today.

Gridiron Gridlock

Today's American football players are known for their strength, athleticism and fearlessness – there's no denying football is an aggressive and dangerous contact sport. However, the NFL's finest experience nothing compared to the unadulterated carnage that existed on the gridirons of the early 1900s. The forward pass was illegal, so players locked arms and formed mass battering rams to get the ball up the field, and gang tackles were common. The players wore little in the way of protective clothing or body armour, resulting in crushed skulls, broken ribs and severed spinal cords. The injuries were so frequent and so severe that newspapers campaigned for high schools and colleges to give up the sport altogether.

The Bloodbath at Hampden Park

Roosevelt had good reason to be worried – after a bloody game between Harvard and Yale in 1894, the sport was banned by administrators for two years. Known as the 'Hampden Park Bloodbath,' more than five players were hospitalised during the game, which saw players receive head injuries, as well as broken noses, collarbones and legs. The bloodshed continued off the pitch, with violent fights breaking out between rival fans. After the two-year hiatus, the game wasn't put on hold again until World War I.

Preparing for Battle

President Roosevelt felt that football was an important part of American life and that being on a football team and playing the sport was akin to being on the battlefield. He supported the masculine, heavy-handed nature of the

game, but he realised something had to change if the sport was to maintain its popularity. In 1905 he'd invited the head football coaches from Harvard, Princeton and Yale to the White House to encourage them to clean up the game. Despite his efforts, fatalities rose. In the same year, Roosevelt's own son, who was on the football team at Harvard, had his nose broken in a game.

The deaths of at least 18 players and nearly 150 serious injuries in 1905 was the final straw for some schools, including Stanford, California, Columbia and Duke, which either switched to rugby or dropped football altogether. Fearing his own alma mater, Harvard, would be next to abandon his beloved sport, Roosevelt urged the remaining football authorities to make some serious rule changes. Initially, the forward pass was legalised and the mass formations were banned, while further restrictions and changes made in 1909 led to the creation of the sport recognised today. It would be a number of years until helmets and body padding became mandatory for players in the NFL.

'After a bloody game between Harvard and Yale in 1894, the sport was banned by administrators for two years.'

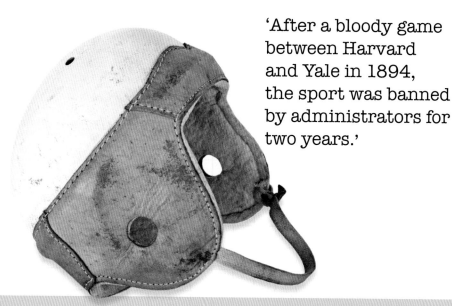

Why is the Tour de France's yellow jersey yellow?

You don't need to be a big fan of the Tour de France to know that the cyclist leading the overall race wears the yellow jersey – the garment has become synonymous with the sport. But it wasn't always so. Despite the race being around since 1903, the jersey didn't make its first appearance until 1919.

Making His Mark

The first person to wear the yellow jersey, or *maillot jaune*, was French rider Eugène Christophe. The year was 1919, and it was the first time the Tour had taken place since 1914. World War I had brought destruction and devastation to the people of France, and it was decided that the Tour, which had quickly become a hugely popular event, was what was needed to boost the morale of the people. While today's riders covet the yellow jersey, in 1919 Eugène Christophe was less keen, claiming it made him an easier mark for the other riders. Unfortunately, despite wearing the jersey for 10 of the Tour's 15 stages (there are now 21 one-day segments completed over 23 days), Christophe lost the winning spot to Belgian Firmin Lambot, finishing third on the podium.

Why Yellow?

The Tour was put on by *L'Auto*, a sports magazine that began the stage race as a way to boost circulation. Prior to 1919, the race leader would wear a yellow armband to signify his position. But this made it hard for fans to pick him out from the side of the road, so it was suggested to the magazine's editor, Henri Desgrange, that a coloured jersey might make more

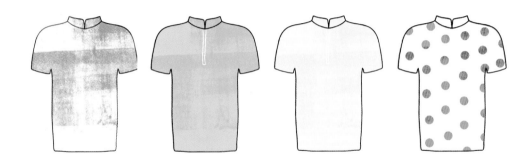

sense. It's believed that yellow was chosen to reflect the colour of the paper that *L'Auto* was printed on, but legend also has it that Desgrange needed 15 jerseys – one for each stage of the race – and that the supplier only had that number available in yellow, the least popular colour.

Jersey Rules

The yellow jersey is worn by whichever rider is leading the general classification after the previous day's stage. In other words, they are the leader of the overall time ranking when their times from all completed stages are added together. Even if you don't win the overall race, if you've worn a yellow jersey at any point in the Tour, you get to keep it as a souvenir. But wearing the jersey doesn't guarantee victory. Fabian Cancellara has spent 29 days wearing the yellow jersey, across six Tours, without ever winning the overall race.

COLOURS OF THE TOUR

The yellow jersey might be the most recognisable, but it's not the only special jersey that features in the Tour. Continuing in order of jersey ranking, there's the green jersey, awarded to the rider leading the points classification; the polka-dot jersey, worn by the 'King of the Mountains' for the rider with the best climber ranking; and the white jersey, worn by the highest general classification-ranked rider under the age of 26. If a rider is leading in more than one classification, he wears whichever jersey is ranked higher.

What do you do in a *dojo*?

Kyudo, meaning 'the way of the bow', is an ancient Japanese discipline dating to 250 BCE. It is practised in a special hall called a *kyudojo*, or *dojo* for short, and the process of learning and preparing to shoot a bow is meditative and spiritual – it's heavily influenced by Shinto and Zen Buddhism.

The Way of the Bow

There are eight stages to shooting a bow using the *kyudo* technique, and even the correct stance can take a long time to master. Archers must spread their feet the distance of one arrow length, called *yazuka*, with their big toes lined up with the centre of the target. *Hikiwake*, meaning 'drawing the bow', sees the archer draw the bow at forehead height, before lowering it to mouth level to release. *Dojo* members take it in turns to shoot at the target – the least experienced go first, followed by the highly skilled archers.

ARCHERY AT THE OLYMPICS

Target archery has been included in every Olympic Games since 1972. Archers have just 40 seconds to shoot six arrows at a target positioned 70 metres away – about three-quarters of a football pitch. The target's central circle, the bullseye, measures just 12.2 centimetres across. When the bow is released, the arrow travels at speeds of 240 kilometres per hour. Olympic archers use a recurve bow, where both ends of the bow curve away from the archer when it's unstrung.

SPORTS

You've put the training in; now it's time to stretch your muscles and claim the title by taking this quiz!

Questions

1. Basketball was originally played using two peach baskets instead of hoops and nets – true or false?

2. What breakfast food inspired the soles of Nike's first shoe?

3. In archery, what is the target's central circle called?

4. Natural waves created by rising oceans washing inland up a gradually narrowing river are known as tidal yawns, tidal bores or tidal stretches?

5. With which sport would you associate a 'birdie', 'eagle' and 'albatross'?

6. What is BASE jumping?

7. Yellow tennis balls were introduced after research showed players could hit them faster – true or false?

8. Which American college sport was banned for two years after the 1894 'Hampden Park Bloodbath'?

9. What did Jesse Owens need a trowel for when he walked out onto the running tracks in the 1930s?

10. The rider leading the general classification in the Tour de France wears a polka-dot jersey – true or false?

Turn to page 248 for the answers.

DO SELF-TANNING PRODUCTS PROTECT YOUR SKIN FROM THE SUN'S RAYS?

WHAT'S THE WORLD'S MOST DANGEROUS CHEMICAL?

WHY IS YAWNING CONTAGIOUS?

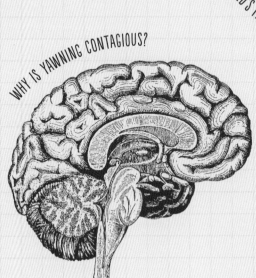

WHAT MAKES BACON SMELL SO DELICIOUS?

WHY IS CHOCOLATE BAD FOR DOGS?

WHAT HAS BLUE BLOOD?

SCIENCE

What's the world's most dangerous chemical?

New chemicals are being created and discovered on a regular basis. Often, scientists can guess at the reactions that will occur, based on a chemical's properties. Other times, as was the case with the following contenders for the world's scariest chemical, they get a nasty surprise.

TOXIC

Substance N-o Way

If the Nazis considered something too dangerous, you know to be very, very afraid. Chlorine trifluoride (ClF_3) was discovered in the 1930s in Germany, and a few years later it became a subject of study at the Kaiser Wilhelm Institute, where the Third Reich conducted a number of scientific experiments. Dubbed *N-stoff* or 'substance N' by those researching it, there was no denying the chemical's remarkable properties. It produces a toxic gas at boiling point, which is a mere 11.75°C; it ignites easily and burns at over 2,400°C ; it's highly corrosive; and it explodes on contact with water. The Nazis planned to produce 50 metric tons of substance N every month, and use it to destroy their enemies. One plan involved putting it in flamethrowers to dowse whole cities in the lethal weapon. However, the chemical's volatile nature was also its downfall – it would even eat through the flamethrower before the weapon could be used – so the Nazis only produced about 50 metric tons of the stuff in total. Even the brains at NASA couldn't figure out how to harness its properties. Packing so much power, they thought it might make the perfect propellant for launching rockets, but after a 1950s spillage ate through a steel tank, a concrete floor and about a metre of gravel underneath, they changed their minds.

What's That Smell?

An extremely stinky chemical might not sound scary, but thioacetone (C_3H_6S) was responsible for the evacuation of an entire city. In 1889, scientists in Freiberg, Germany, who were working with the chemical reported 'an offensive smell which spread rapidly over a great area of the town, causing fainting, vomiting and a panic evacuation'. The chemical is so potent that one drop can be smelled from half a kilometre away. In the 1960s, two chemists made the mistake of leaving a stopper off a bottle of the substance while experimenting with it as part of an investigation into new polymers at the Esso Research Station in Abingdon, UK. They couldn't escape the stench and received a deodorant dosing from a waitress when they went out for dinner.

SUPER ACID

Insane explosives and unbearable odours aside, there's nothing more terrifying than a highly corrosive acid. Perhaps the world's strongest is fluoroantimonic acid (H_2FSbF_6). It's so strong it can eat through glass, plastic and any living organism, including bone. That might sound scary, but in order to store it safely you just need a container made from polytetrafluoroethylene, otherwise known as Teflon.

'Thioacetone (C_3H_6S) was responsible for the evacuation of an entire city.'

Why does it hurt so much when you step on a LEGO brick?

We all know how painful it is to accidentally step on a LEGO brick with bare feet. Despite their diminutive size, those teeny plastic building blocks can pack a powerful punch, leaving you hopping around in a rage.

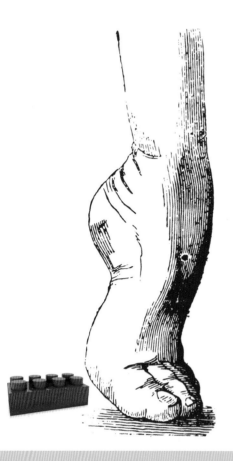

Playing with Pain

When you feel pain, it's thanks to your body's nociceptors – sensory nerve cells that send signals to your spinal cord and brain using nerve fibres. In your skin, you have two different kinds of pain-sensing nerve fibres: C and A-delta. The latter are the sensory nerve fibres that carry acute, piercing pain signals to the brain, usually caused by cold or pressure. A-deltas are the nerve fibers affected when you step on a LEGO brick.

To avoid you having to feel the pain of those little studs digging into your foot for longer than necessary, the A-delta fibres send the message to your spinal cord first, to instigate the withdrawal reflex. The motor neurons in your foot are then triggered to move from the source of the pain, even before your brain knows it's happened.

'When you feel pain, it's thanks to your body's nociceptors.'

Super-Strong Toys

When you step on the brick, the force of your entire body weight is concentrated on the part of the brick you hit – usually those sharp edges. The strength of the ABS plastic means it doesn't give under your weight. The full pressure load is felt by the dense concentration of the thousands of sensory receptors in your foot. Ouch! If you think being heavier might help you in this situation, enabling you to crush the little brick under your weight, you need to understand just how strong LEGO bricks are.

A 2012 experiment using a servo-hydraulic testing machine determined that the force required on one small two-stud by two-stud LEGO brick to make it collapse in on itself was 4,240 newtons. To recreate that force in mass, you would need to weigh 430 kilos – the equivalent of a grand piano or a large horse. LEGO bricks are so light, you'd need to stack 375,000 on top of that single brick to have the same effect. That's why enthusiasts are able to build giant LEGO towers over 30 metres tall without seeing the bottom crumble under the pressure.

LEARNING ABOUT LEGO

Plastic LEGO bricks were first produced in the late 1940s when the Danish company acquired a plastic injection-moulding machine. But it was the switch to acrylonitrile butadiene styrene (ABS) in 1962 that really began to set the company's building bricks apart from its rivals'. The three monomers bonded together in ABS give the plastic its key attributes: acrylonitrile makes it strong; butadiene makes it resistant, so it doesn't snap when you pull LEGO bricks apart; and styrene makes it smooth and shiny. As ABS was relatively inexpensive at the time, easy to mould in small amounts, and more colourfast and durable than the cellulose acetate LEGO had been using, making the switch was a no-brainer. LEGO has been made from ABS ever since.

Why is yawning contagious?

Seeing a picture of a yawn or even talking about yawning is enough to provoke a gaping-mouth stretch of significant proportions in some people – and it seems that the more empathetic you are, the more likely you are to launch into a yawn whenever you see others doing so.

It's Catching

There are a number of theories as to why humans yawn when they see others doing it, but mimicry is one that holds a lot of weight. As social creatures, empathy – the ability to feel and understand the emotions of others – plays an important part in our social cohesion. When we see others smiling or laughing, we tend to smile or laugh, and the same is true for frowning or sad expressions. Research at the Yerkes National Primate Research Center at Emory University, United States, indicates that contagious yawning may just be a by-product of an empathetic nature.

About 60–70% of people are susceptible to contagious yawning, and the research shows it occurs most often in individuals who score highly on empathetic tests. Scans of the brain show that the areas activated during contagious yawning are the same areas involved in the processing of our own emotions and those of other people. And we're not the only species to do it. This catching behaviour has been observed in chimpanzees and bonobos.

The Yawning Myth

Being tired or bored, and the sight of someone else doing it, can all trigger a yawn, but what does the body get in return for this often socially awkward response? The reason often cited is

that it's our body's way of increasing oxygen to the bloodstream. But science has turned up no evidence as yet that yawning increases the levels of oxygen in the blood. Other theories suggest that it's a primitive form of communication used to alert the group to tiredness, setting everyone's bodies to the same sleep pattern; or that the strenuous stretch of the face makes you more alert when you're sleepy or more focused when you're distracted.

COOL OFF

However, the one prevailing school of thought is that yawning helps to regulate brain temperature. A 2007 study at SUNY College, Oneonta, United States, found that when a hot pack was held to a participant's forehead, they yawned 41% of the time, compared to 9% for cold packs. The brain heats up more than other organs, and the gaping mouth of a yawn means a bigger gulp of air is inhaled, which travels to our upper nasal and oral cavities. The blood vessels in these areas head straight up to the brain, cooling it off. The jaw stretch also increases the rate of blood flow, so the brain can benefit from that rush of cool air more efficiently. Before we fall asleep and when we wake up our brain and body temperatures are at their highest, which would explain why we tend to yawn most at these times.

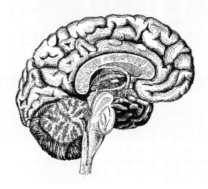

Why is chocolate bad for dogs?

Cocoa contains a molecule called theobromine, which is very toxic to dogs. Chemically speaking, it's similar to caffeine. Consumed in small doses, this molecule can increase your heart rate and the amount of oxygen and nutrients to your brain. But how does it affect dogs?

Candy Catastrophe

Despite being man's best friend, dogs are very different from us – their bodies don't metabolise theobromine very well. This means the effects that are minimal to us last a lot longer in a dog's central nervous system. When dogs eat chocolate, they can develop theobromine poisoning. The symptoms, which include a high temperature, seizures, vomiting, heavy panting and diarrhoea, can take up to 12 hours to set in. Dark chocolate (with cocoa percentages of 70% and above), baking chocolate and cocoa powder have higher concentrations of theobromine, so are more harmful to dogs. For a dog weighing 20 kilos to consume a deadly dose of theobromine, it would have to devour over 3 kilos of milk chocolate. Considering your average candy bar weighs about 50 grams, Fido would have to gobble down about 60 bars for it to have a lethal effect.

FREAKISH FELINES

Despite its toxic nature, most dogs love the taste of chocolate and can't get enough, with small dogs more likely to feel the effects. Their purring pals, however, are unlikely to seek out the deadly delicacy. Why? That's because the taste receptors in cats' tongues aren't configured like ours or dogs' – they can't taste anything sweet, because they lack one of the genes required to do so.

Why does cutting an onion make you cry?

When tears are streaming from your eyes next time you're making dinner, it might seem as though the onions are exacting their revenge for sacrificing them for your meal, but in actual fact that gas is created by the sulphur that onions absorb from the soil.

Sobbing Sulphur

Slicing into an onion splits open its cells, causing a chemical reaction that releases a gas called syn-Propanethial-S-oxide – a combination of special enzymes and sulfenic acid. When the sensory nerves in the front of your eyes detect this invasive compound, a message is sent to your central nervous system, which you experience as a burning sensation. A signal is then sent to your tear-producing glands to wash out the irritant gas, and you get all weepy – but when you banish the pesky onions to a hot pan, the heat deactivates the enzymes.

It's thought that this lachrymator gas is produced to deter the plant's herbivore predators. Onion tears can be avoided by chilling the vegetable in the refrigerator first – the cold impacts some of the onion's gas-inducing compounds. There is an upside to the tears, though: those sulphur compounds give onions their unique flavour.

THE 'NO-TEARS' ONION

One British farmer made headlines in 2015 when he announced the development of a red onion variety that does not trigger tears. Twenty years in the making, the farmer claimed the 'Sweet Red' variety had lower pungency levels than regular onions, making it easier on your eyes – and on your breath!

Is the periodic table complete?

In late 2015, scientists rejoiced at the completion of the seventh row of the periodic table of elements after the results of years of experiments were confirmed by the International Union of Pure and Applied Chemistry (IUPAC). This opened up the invitation to begin the next row – but will scientists eventually stop discovering new elements?

A Seat at the Table

The periodic table organises elements by rows and columns. The rows, called periods, are based on the elements' atomic numbers – in other words, the number of protons in an atom's nucleus – and the columns, called groups, are based on the orbits of their outermost electrons. These orbits inform the personality of the element, so elements in the same group tend to behave similarly. For example, all the elements in group one are alkali metals that are soft and highly reactive, such as lithium, sodium and rubidium.

PERIODIC TABLE

1 **H** 1.0079 Hydrogen																	2 **He** 4.0026 Helium
3 **Li** 1.941 Lithium	4 **Be** 9.0122 Beryllium											5 **B** 10.811 Boron	6 **C** 12.011 Carbon	7 **N** 14.007 Nitrogen	8 **O** 15.999 Oxygen	9 **F** 18.998 Fluorine	10 **Ne** 20.180 Neon
11 **Na** 22.990 Sodium	12 **Mg** 24.305 Magnesium											13 **Al** 26.982 Aluminium	14 **Si** 28.086 Silicon	15 **P** 30.974 Phosphorus	16 **S** 32.065 Sulfur	17 **Cl** 35.453 Chlorine	18 **Ar** 39.948 Argon
19 **K** 39.098 Potassium	20 **Ca** 40.078 Calcium	21 **Sc** 44.956 Scandium	22 **Ti** 47.867 Titanium	23 **V** 50.942 Vanadium	24 **Cr** 51.996 Chromium	25 **Mn** 54.938 Manganese	26 **Fe** 55.845 Iron	27 **Co** 58.933 Cobalt	28 **Ni** 58.693 Nickel	29 **Cu** 63.546 Copper	30 **Zn** 65.39 Zinc	31 **Ga** 69.723 Gallium	32 **Ge** 1.0579 Germanium	33 **As** 74.922 Arsenic	34 **Se** 78.96 Selenium	35 **Br** 79.904 Bromine	36 **Kr** 83.80 Krypton
37 **Rb** 85.468 Rubidium	38 **Sr** 87.62 Strontium	39 **Y** 88.906 Yttrium	40 **Zr** 91.224 Zirconium	41 **Nb** 92.906 Niobium	42 **Mo** 95.94 Molybdenum	43 **Tc** 98 Technetium	44 **Ru** 101.07 Ruthenium	45 **Rh** 102.91 Rhodium	46 **Pd** 106.42 Palladium	47 **Ag** 107.87 Silver	48 **Cd** 112.41 Cadmium	49 **In** 114.82 Indium	50 **Sn** 118.71 Tin	51 **Sb** 121.76 Antimony	52 **Te** 127.60 Tellurium	53 **I** 126.90 Iodine	54 **Xe** 131.29 Xenon
55 **Cs** 132.91 Caesium	56 **Ba** 137.33 Barium	57 - 71 **La - Lu**	72 **Hf** 178.49 Hafnium	73 **Ta** 180.95 Tantalum	74 **W** 183.84 Tungsten	75 **Re** 186.21 Rhenium	76 **Os** 190.23 Osmium	77 **Ir** 192.22 Iridium	78 **Pt** 195.08 Platinum	79 **Au** 196.97 Gold	80 **Hg** 200.59 Mercury	81 **Tl** 204.38 Thallium	82 **Pb** 207.2 Lead	83 **Bi** 208.98 Bismuth	84 **Po** 209 Polonium	85 **At** 210 Astatine	86 **Rn** 222 Radon
87 **Fr** 223 Francium	88 **Ra** 226 Radium	89 - 103 **Ac - Lr**	104 **Rf** 261 Rutherfordium	105 **Db** 262 Dubnium	106 **Sg** 266 Seaborgium	107 **Bh** 264 Bohrium	108 **Hs** 269 Hassium	109 **Mt** 268 Meitnerium	110 **Uun** 271 Ununnilium	111 **Uuu** 272 Unununium	112 **Uub** 285 Ununbium	113 **Uut** 1.0079 Ununtrium	114 **Uuq** 289 Ununquadium	115 **Uup** 288 Ununpentium	116 **Uuh** 292 Ununhexium	117 **Uus** Ununseptium	118 **Uuo** Ununoctium

LANTHANIDE SERIES

57 **La** 138.91 Lanthanide	58 **Ce** 140.12 Cerium	59 **Pr** 140.91 Praseodymium	60 **Nd** 144.24 Neodymium	61 **Pm** 145 Promethium	62 **Sm** 150.36 Samarium	63 **Eu** 151.96 Europium	64 **Gd** 157.25 Gadolinium	65 **Tb** 158.93 Terbium	66 **Dy** 162.5 Dysprosium	67 **Ho** 164.93 Holmium	68 **Er** 1.0079 Erbium	69 **Tm** 168.93 Thulium	70 **Yb** 173.04 Ytterbium	71 **Lu** 1.0079 Lutetium

ACTINIDE SERIES

89 **Ac** 227 Actinide	90 **Th** 232.04 Thorium	91 **Pa** 231.04 Protactinium	92 **U** 238.03 Uranium	93 **Np** 237 Neptunium	94 **Pu** 244 Plutonium	95 **Am** 243 Americium	96 **Cm** 247 Curium	97 **Bk** 247 Berkelium	98 **Cf** 251 Californium	99 **Es** 252 Einsteinium	100 **Fm** 257 Fermium	101 **Md** 258 Mendelevium	102 **No** 259 Nobelium	103 **Lr** 1.0079 Lawrencium

Uranium, with an atomic number of 92, is the last element on the table that's stable enough to occur naturally on Earth. Every other element beyond it is only studied by smashing together lighter atoms to create heavier ones, and then searching through the decay to identify heavier elements. Scientists have calculated that they may be able to discover elements up to an atomic number of 173, but this process currently has its limitations. It's possible that much heavier elements exist inside stars and elsewhere in the universe, making the table far from complete.

Swedish Symbols

Prior to the systematic classification in place today, various symbols were used for different elements, but as the number of known elements grew, a more ordered method became essential. Swedish chemist Jöns Jacob Berzelius assigned many of the symbol letters in the early 19th century, and his method became accepted around the world. Most elements' symbols are made from the first letter or first two letters of their name, such as oxygen (O), nitrogen (N), aluminum (Al) and nickel (Ni). But where elements have the same first two initials, they deviate from this pattern: for example, calcium (Ca), caesium (Cs) and cadmium (Cd). Some symbols are derived from the element's Latin name. Gold, for example, has the symbol Au, from the Latin *aurum*, and copper is Cu, from *cuprum*.

NEW DISCOVERIES

It's IUPAC's job to make the final decision about the names and symbols for each new element, and in the last few years they've been busy adding four new elements to the table. The discovery of 113, 115, 117 and 118 by scientists in Russia, Japan and the United States was confirmed at the end of 2015, completing the seventh row of the table. They have since been officially named nihonium (Nh), moscovium (Mc), tennessine (Ts) and oganesson (Og), respectively. The discovery of these synthetic elements took years and was only possible in a laboratory, where they existed for a fraction of a second. Work is already underway to discover 119 and 120.

What makes bacon smell so delicious?

Bacon is the one thing many vegetarians would shun their meat-free lives for. And it's no surprise – the distinct aroma of frying bacon draws people to the kitchen like moths to a flame. Scientists have found that over 150 chemicals combine to create the unique smell that gets your mouth watering.

Browning Brilliance

When bacon is sizzling in the pan, there's a whole lot of chemistry going on. First, there's the Maillard reaction – it's what makes things turn brown when you cook them. It's caused when the bacon is heated and the amino acids it contains react with the natural sugars, breaking them down. Other compounds are given off from the breaking down of bacon fat.

The Ultimate Cure

One thing that sets the smell of fried bacon apart from other cooked pork products is the fact that it's been cured. While aroma compounds such as pyridine, pyrazine and furans are found in both fried bacon and fried pork loin, these meaty-smelling molecules are dramatically increased with the presence of nitrites, which are used in the curing process of bacon. When the nitrites in bacon fat are heated, they create more nitrogen-containing compounds found exclusively in bacon, including 2,5-dimethylpyrazine, 2,3-dimethylpyrazine, 2-ethyl-5-methylpyrazine and 2-ethyl-3,5-dimethylpyrazine. Scientists believe it's the combination of these that give bacon its unique aroma.

Taste Sensation

However, bacon's draw is not just its smell. The taste is what keeps people coming back for more. The flavour, like the aroma, is created by a combination of elements. One of the major factors is the result of the pork belly's fat breaking down. Classes of molecules, such as aldehydes, furans and ketones, are created by the breakdown of fatty acids in the muscle tissue and combine

to create the unique flavour. If any were missing, bacon would not taste as it does. But not all bacon is alike, and the breed of pig the bacon is derived from, and what that pig was fed on, affect the type of fatty acids that are present, and therefore the molecules that result when they're broken down.

A Mouthful of Mouthfeel

Finally, bacon's draw is something known as 'mouthfeel' – the way certain foods feel in the mouth. Crispy bacon provides a stark contrast to the foods it's usually served with – pancakes, eggs and potatoes. This texture combination satisfies the brain's craving for novelty, increasing the amount of pleasure you experience when you eat it. The melt-in-the-mouth nature of bacon also makes it very moreish. Known as 'vanishing caloric density', your brain is tricked into thinking you're eating fewer calories than you are, urging you to eat more.

What has blue blood?

The term 'blue blood' refers to a person of noble birth. It's believed to have originated from the Spanish term *sangre azul*, used to describe the rich, powerful Castile families in medieval Spain whose relatively pale skin, unlike that of their Moorish enemies, showed off their 'blue' veins. But does anything actually have blue blood?

Red-Blooded Mammals

Like most other vertebrates, our blood contains a protein called haemoglobin, which helps carry oxygen around the body. Haemoglobin is made up of bound iron atoms, whose structure absorbs light of particular wavelengths, which is why it looks red. However, when you look at your veins through your skin, your blood looks blue. So why do your veins look blue through your skin? The blue appearance is because red light can penetrate deeper into tissue than blue light, meaning more blue light is reflected into your eyes. The actual colour of this deoxygenated venous blood is a darker red than the oxygenated blood in your arteries.

Feeling Blue

Haemoglobin is the reason for our red blood, but some other animals have different oxygen-carrying proteins in their blood cells, which leads to a rainbow of different blood colours. Rather than haemoglobin, crustaceans, squid, octopuses, spiders and a number of molluscs have haemocyanin in their blood. Haemocyanin doesn't bind to red blood cells like haemoglobin, but instead floats freely in the blood. It also contains copper atoms, instead

of iron. These differences mean their blood is colourless when deoxygenated, and blue when oxygenated.

Bloody Rainbow

Blue isn't the only unexpected blood colour found inside organisms. Despite seeming like something out of a horror film, green blood is found in some worms and leeches, and purple blood is the norm for some other worms. The former is caused by the presence of chlorocruorin, which turns deoxygentated blood light green and oxygenated blood darker green. In high concentration, however, it appears light red. Purple blood is caused by the respiratory pigment hemerythrin and is found in peanut worms, brachiopods and the hilariously named penis worm.

FROZEN BLOOD

The haemocyanin in Antarctic octopuses' blood isn't just for show. They've evolved that way to cope with the freezing temperatures, which range from −1.8°C to 2°C. The icy water makes it harder to transport oxygen around the body, but the copper-containing pigment is more efficient at keeping their blood oxygenated in the cold. A study showed that there is significantly more haemocyanin in the blood of Antarctic octopuses compared with their warmer-water cousins, but that – unlike many fish species – they are able to oxygenate their blood in warmer climes, too, meaning they are better prepared for the effects of climate change.

Do self-tanning products protect your skin from the Sun's rays?

We've long been warned about the dangers of sun exposure, prompting us to seek an alternative to achieve that glowing golden tone. Today's self-tanning products are a far cry from their streaky orange ancestors, but at what cost? What are they doing to your skin? And do they provide protection from the Sun's harmful rays?

Mythical Barrier

Many people misguidedly think that the layer of tanned skin they obtain from using a self-tanning lotion or spray acts as a barrier, protecting their skin from the sun. But most topical self-tanning products only contain SPF 2 or 3. SPF stands for 'sun protection factor' and the figure refers to the fraction of UV rays that will reach the skin if wearing the product, in this case, a half or a third. This is inefficient protection on its own.

How Does Fake Tan Work?

On the surface of your skin is the stratum corneum. This outermost layer comprises dead skin cells and provides a natural barrier to the new, living cells underneath. One of its components is keratin protein, which gives skin its structure. Most tanning products contain an active ingredient called dihydroxyacetone (DHA), which reacts

with the amino acids in keratin protein and eventually forms brown compounds called melanoidins – the effect is a gradual browning of the skin cells. This reaction is called the Maillard reaction and is similar to what happens when you cook meat or toast bread. It takes a while to occur, which is why you can't see the full effects of a tanning product until a few hours afterwards, and the reaction can last up to three days.

Fake It Till You Make It

Most tanning products contain 2–5% DHA. The more DHA you apply to the skin, the darker it will become. But then, as your skin replaces the dead skin cells on the surface with new dead skin cells, you'll start to notice the colour fading. Fake tans can't last longer than about a week, purely for the fact that the dead skin cells will be shed regardless. The reaction can also be affected by the amount of water the skin comes into contact with, which is why it's recommended not to wash in the few hours after applying a product.

More Harm Than Good

Some studies have suggested that using these products may actually increase the amount of damage your skin can sustain from exposure to the sun. One study found that in the 24 hours after DHA application, three times more free radicals were formed on the skin during sun exposure. But the DHA concentration was 20%, considerably more than the maximum 5% found in most products. Free radicals are atoms missing an electron. They bond to healthy cells to try to steal an electron from them, causing a domino effect of damage, in this case to the skin. They're all around us, but their production is triggered by air pollution, smoking and the sun, among other things.

How do forensic investigators find traces of blood (and horseradish) at a crime scene?

Crime-show junkies know that mopping up a pool of blood is never going to fully cover a murderer's tracks. When TV investigators arrive at the crime scene, they usually spray everything with a liquid, illuminating blood stains the criminal thought no one would ever find. So what's in the spray bottle?

Illuminating the Problem

The bottle usually contains luminol – a powdery compound that's made up of nitrogen, hydrogen, oxygen and carbon. It's mixed together with other chemicals, including hydrogen peroxide and sodium hydroxide, and sprayed where investigators think traces of blood might be hiding. A chemical reaction is caused when the luminol is sprayed on haemoglobin – the oxygen-carrying protein in blood. The chemicals break down the molecules in the haemoglobin, which emit energy in the form of light photons, creating a pale blue luminescence when the room is dark. Even if the blood has been washed away, traces of up to one part per million can be detected by luminol.

True Crime

In reality, unlike the glow you normally see on TV, that pale blue evidence will only glow for around 30 seconds, and spraying luminol can also smear blood impressions, damaging evidence. Despite its effectiveness, the method is not foolproof, as other things can be the catalyst for the same glowing reaction. Chemicals in bleach, urine with blood in it, faeces and even enzymes in horseradish can cause a false positive.

Why do the leaves change colour in autumn?

Every autumn, almost like clockwork, the leaves on the trees are transformed from their usual luscious greens to a warming palette of yellows, oranges and reds. Behind this autumnal artistry lies some clever chemistry.

Going Green

Chlorophyll is the chemical compound that creates the characteristic green colour present in most leaves. This is an important component in photosynthesis – the process by which plants convert energy from sunlight into carbon dioxide, and water into sugars. As winter approaches and the days get darker, sunshine is in short supply, and so the production of chlorophyll slows down. Existing chlorophyll in the leaves decomposes. But the change from green to yellow, orange or red is not the chlorophyll decomposing, but rather the other compounds in the leaves, always present but usually less dominant, showing their true colours.

Seeing Red

Other pigment families found in leaves include carotenoids and flavonoids, which create yellow hues, while carotenoids also lead to oranges and reds. These decompose more slowly than chlorophyll, so it becomes possible to see them as the chlorophyll diminishes. In plants with red or purple leaves, the dominant pigment compounds are anthocyanins. These aren't typically found all year-round, but their production is triggered by an increased concentration of sugar in the leaves, caused by darker days. The advantages of anthocyanins are not fully understood, but theories suggest their antioxidant properties protect the plant as it prepares for winter.

Can you unboil an egg?

Scientists might not have figured out how we can live on the Moon, but they have solved one of breakfast's most important mysteries. Yes, it is possible to unboil an egg – at least, the white of it.

How Do You Like Your Eggs?

Eggs are protein-rich, and these proteins, like others, are made up of amino acids – building blocks arranged in a specific way, giving the protein its unique shape and useful properties. When these proteins are subjected to an increase in temperature, the connections are disrupted, causing the protein to unravel and tangle. This is what causes an egg to go from clear to white when boiled.

At the University of California, Irvine, United States, research chemists added a urea substance to cooked egg whites. This waste product chewed away at the whites, returning the solid egg to a liquid. They then used a special vortex fluid device, which stressed the proteins back into their original formation.

Protein Power

These scientists weren't trying to figure this out just for fun. Their research has lots of underlying implications for cutting the costs of food production and for cancer treatments, among other things. Vast amounts of money are spent on reversing the misfolding process that occurs when proteins are formed, or preventing it in the first place. For example, to make cancer antibodies, scientists use hamster ovary cells, which don't misfold proteins. This new method is fast, reduces waste and has the potential to save industries the £125 billion spent on proteins each year.

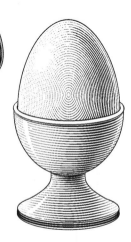

SCIENCE

Ready to win first prize at the science fair? Sort your protons from your electrons, don your lab coat and prepare to unleash your inner genius.

Questions

1. The Maillard reaction makes food turn what colour when you cook it?

2. What does SPF (on tanning product packaging) stand for?

3. Does the production of chlorophyll in leaves speed up or slow down in the winter?

4. LEGO bricks are made from ABS – this is a type of what?

5. Yawning increases the levels of oxygen in the blood – true or false?

6. Which is more harmful to dogs: dark chocolate, milk chocolate or white chocolate?

7. Which dictatorial regime experimented with substance N in the 1930s?

8. Is the periodic table complete?

9. Haemoglobin is a protein found in blood that makes it appear which colour?

10. Luminol spray shows crime scene investigators where ketchup has been – true or false?

Turn to page 248 for the answers.

WHO ARE THE MOST WELL-PAID PETS IN CINEMA HISTORY?

WHO WAS THE WORLD'S FIRST ACTOR?

DOES A SHOW HAVE TO BE ON BROADWAY TO BE A BROADWAY SHOW?

WHY DID FILMMAKERS ASK BRUCE LEE TO PUNCH MORE SLOWLY?

FILM AND THEATRE

207

Which was Shakespeare's most successful play in his lifetime?

In England, prior to 1576, actors performed in college halls, private houses and inns, but the construction of theatres such as the Rose and the Globe – in which William Shakespeare himself owned shares – provided dedicated spaces where up to 3,000 people could watch a production together.

History Buffs

Unlike today, when *A Midsummer Night's Dream*, *Hamlet*, *Macbeth* and *Romeo and Juliet* top lists of the most performed and most popular Shakespeare plays, it was his history plays that were the most sought after in his own lifetime. The two most-published plays between the 1590s and 1630s were *Henry IV Part I*, published 11 times, and *Richard III*, published 10 times. Shakespeare was writing about powerful historical figures and events not long in the past. Richard III, for example, died in 1485, heralding the end of the Wars of the Roses and the start of the mighty Tudor dynasty. His historical figures included Queen Elizabeth I, one of Shakespeare's chief patrons. Being a Shakespeare history fan in the 16th and 17th centuries was not too dissimilar from modern audiences being enthralled by dramas set in World War I or the reign of Queen Victoria.

Modern audiences are less likely to know the difference between their Henrys, while 'To be or not to be', uttered by a fictional Danish prince, has become the best-known line of Shakespeare's work. Over four hundred years after Shakespeare's death, *Hamlet* has been translated into more than 75 languages, even *Star Trek*'s Klingon.

Cheap as Beer

Plays were performed most afternoons, meaning up to 20,000 people a week paid to go and see a show (a huge number when you consider the population of London was around 250,000). As a result, plays only had very short runs and were quickly replaced, meaning it was hard for anything to be a runaway hit like West End or Broadway shows today. That said, while nothing was technically a

'box office' smash, the term is derived from the box that audiences had to deposit their money into when they entered the theatre or sometimes to get to the good seats. And the theatre wasn't just for the rich; you could watch a show for just one 'penny', although you'd have to stand in the open-air 'yard' area that surrounded the stage. If you think a penny doesn't sound like much, you'd be right. For the same price you could buy a loaf of bread or two-thirds of a gallon of beer.

GLOBAL FAILURE

While his audiences were big fans of his 10 history plays, Shakespeare might have had a less favourable response after one particular performance of his last, *Henry VIII*. During a 1613 production, the Globe Theatre came to an untimely end when a stage cannon ignited the thatched roof, burning the whole building to the ground.

Why are all Kabuki actors men?

Kabuki is a traditional Japanese performance art. It dates from the early 17th century, and is believed to have originated with the performances of a female dancer – which is strange, seeing as all the contemporary performers are men.

Sex on the Stage

The word *kabuki* comes from *kabukimono* – a word used to describe people who dressed in extreme clothing and did shocking or unspeakable things. In modern Japanese, the word's three characters mean 'song', 'dance', and 'skill'. The first historical reference to Kabuki can be linked to a woman called Izumo no Okuni. While not a lot is known about her, she is credited with inventing a dance called *kabuki odori* with a troupe of other women performers. This entertainment was meant for the common man, and it was brash, flashy and erotic.

Naturally, there were sex workers (*youjyo*) who also engaged in Kabuki performances. These were known as *youjyo kabuki*, and soon the art form became too controversial for the Japanese government; in 1629 they banned women from performing in them. Teenage boys (*wakashu*) soon took up women's places in what was then known as *wakashu kabuki*, not that this did anything to curb the prostitution and violence associated with the shows. By 1652, the government had outlawed them, too; it was a ban that took over a decade to come into effect, due to Kabuki's popularity.

It's a Man's World

Since then, men have played all the characters. Their physicality, mannerisms, costumes and make-up help the audience to know the characters being portrayed. The make-up style used is known as *kumadori* and is very symbolic. The less human a character is, such as for demons and spirits, the more unusual their make-up. Good characters traditionally have red make-up, their enemies have blue make-up, and brown make-up is reserved for goblins and demons.

It's Show Time

In 2005, Kabuki was recognised by UNESCO as a Masterpiece of the Oral and Intangible Heritage of Humanity, joining practices from around the world with important cultural and historical significance. There are two main types of Kabuki – *kyōgen* and *buyō*. The former is more akin to a play, with the story based on historical events or a fictional tale. The latter is more of a dance performance. Unlike traditional

Western theatre, Kabuki bears some resemblance to British pantomime, where the actors and the audience interact throughout the show. Audience members are known to call out actors' names and clap along, and the actors regularly perform among the audience. Originally, Kabuki shows would run throughout the day, so spectators might watch only a portion of the programme and could come and go as they pleased.

'Good characters traditionally have red make-up; their enemies have blue.'

Who are the most well-paid pets in cinema history?

Dogs are easy to train, eager to please and adorable to boot, so unsurprisingly, man's best friend has featured in films since filmmaking began. And while most pooches pick up only a few hundred quid a day for being on set, one of cinema's earliest stars earned more than many of her human colleagues.

There's No Place Like Bone

Terry, the cairn terrier who played Toto in 1939's *The Wizard of Oz* alongside Judy Garland, was paid $125 per week to play Dorothy's loyal pet. The actors who played the Munchkins, however, were on about $50 per week. Adjusted for inflation, Terry was earning about $2,200 per week – more than many Americans at that time. She also starred with Shirley Temple in *Bright Eyes* and went on to feature in *The Women* with Joan Crawford.

Moneyed Mutts

Terry was by no means Hollywood's most well-paid acting dog. Jack Russell terrier Moose appeared in one feature film, as the titular character in *My Dog Skip,* but he made most of his cash

from his ten-year role as Marty Crane's dog, Eddie, in the long-running TV comedy series *Frasier*. He relinquished the part to his son, Enzo, when he retired. He reportedly earned about $10,000 per episode and featured in nearly 200 episodes of the show's 11-year run. But $2 million is peanuts compared to the amount Rin Tin Tin made from his Warner Bros. contract in the 1930s.

BAD MOOD, BIG CHECK

Grumpy Cat, otherwise known as Tardar Sauce, is one of a whole new breed of four-legged fortune-makers. Social media sites and YouTube have spawned an entire industry of furry stars posing and purring for wads of cash. Grumpy Cat, who even has her own agent, reportedly earned her owner close to $100 million in two years, including the earnings from her film debut, *Grumpy Cat's Worst Christmas Ever*. Not bad for a kitty whose main talent is looking miserable.

The Alsatian was a superstar in his own right, with a private chef and his own radio show. He earned $6,000 per week at the height of his popularity, starring in 28 adventure films such as *The Lightning Warrior* and *The Lone Defender*. In today's money, that's around $87,000 per week!

Big at the Box Office

Cats and dogs aren't the only non-human performers to bring in the big bucks. Over the years, filmmakers have paid big money for some truly massive stars, including Bart the Kodiak bear, who appeared alongside Brad Pitt in *Legends of the Fall* and Anthony Hopkins in *The Edge* – performances that earned him $6 million. Bart was born into captivity and when just five weeks old was adopted by his trainers. He grew to nearly 3 metres tall and weighed in at 670 kilos.

Which country produces the most films each year?

In the Western world, people associate the film industry with Hollywood – America's film-producing powerhouse. But while it's true that Hollywood films earn a 66% share of total global box office revenue, the equivalent of nearly £16 billion, the United States is not where the most films are being produced.

Bollywood Boom

India's Bollywood film industry is worth closer to the £1.6 billion mark, but blows the competition out of the water when it comes to volume. Each year, between 1,500 and 2,000 films are produced by the nation's studios, compared to a paltry 691 released by Hollywood in 2015. And if DVD and VHS sales are taken into account, Nigeria's Nollywood comes in second. In 2013, the African nation produced 1,844 films. While many of these are not released theatrically, they contribute to a £2.6 billion industry.

Once Again for the Cheap Seats

So why the difference in revenue? First, there's only one cinema screen per 96,300 people in India, compared to one per 7,800 in the United States. Second, while millions of cinema tickets are sold in India, they cost a lot less than in the United States, so the industry makes less money. For example, in 2012 India sold 2.6 billion tickets, a billion more than were sold in US cinemas, but India made only one-tenth of the US box office takings. There are also films made in over 40 regional languages, meaning more niche audiences, costly production and fewer nationwide blockbusters. Export is a big factor, too – US films make almost 75% of their revenue from other countries, while Indian and Nigerian films' earnings are largely domestic.

Was there really a phantom at the opera in Paris?

Andrew Lloyd Webber's musical *The Phantom of the Opera* is based on a work by Parisian novelist Gaston Leroux. It begins with the line 'The Opera ghost really existed'. Leroux later claimed that the theatrical ghoul was real, and while this has never been proven, the spooky story does have roots in reality.

Murky Depths

Leroux's 1910 Gothic romance, set in the Palais Garnier in Paris, refers to a lake in the building's bowels, beneath the cellars where Erik, the phantom, lives. This creepy 'lake' actually exists. When trying to lay concrete foundations in 1861, it came to light that the building would be set above an arm of the river Seine. After trying and failing to pump the site dry, a large stone water tank was created, covered by a small grate. The pressure prevents any more water from rising up through the foundations, and the tank helps to stabilise the building.

Death by Chandelier

Before becoming a celebrated crime writer, Leroux worked at *Le Matin* as a courtroom reporter. On 21 May 1896, one of the newspaper's headlines read 'Five hundred kilos on a concierge's head'. It referred to an incident the previous evening at the Palais Garnier, where one woman had died and two had been injured after electrical faults caused two 360-kilogram counterweights to fall from the chandelier above the audience during a performance. In the novel's climax, Erik causes a chandelier to fall into the stalls as a distraction so that he can kidnap Christine, the opera-singing heroine.

Who was the world's first actor?

The word 'thespian' has been used in English to describe actors since the late 17th century. Its origins lie in ancient Greece, where on 23 November 534 BCE, a poet named Thespis of Icaria stepped forward to recite the lines of the character Dionysus. In doing so, he became the world's first official actor.

The Chorus Line

Thespis was performing as the leader of a Greek chorus – a group of between 12 and 50 performers who would perform choral hymns, called dithyrambs, dressed in costumes and masks. This particular performance was thought to be part of the City Dionysia, a spring festival celebrated in Athens in honour of Dionysus, the god of wine, fertility and theatre. The procession involved a statue of the god being carried through the streets to a temple at the foot of the Acropolis, as well as sacrificial bulls, and lots of wine. The festival also featured competitions in music, singing, poetry and dance, and Thespis is believed to have been one of the victors.

Standing Out from the Crowd

There is disagreement among scholars about Thespis's involvement in the development of Greek drama, but some believe he was the first to incorporate speeches into choral tragedy performances, with the introduction of a prologue and monologues, changing the face of theatre forever.

'The word "thespian" has been used in English to describe actors since the late 17th century.'

Why did filmmakers ask Bruce Lee to punch more slowly?

Bruce Lee's first major role was as the sidekick Kato in the TV series *The Green Hornet*. His martial arts skills, displayed at Long Beach's International Karate Championships in 1964, had impressed producers – but it clearly hadn't occurred to them that Lee was too fast to capture on film.

Pacy Punching

Original footage of Bruce Lee's full-throttle moves as Kato made it look like he was standing still while his opponents dropped like flies around him – his punches were too fast to be picked up by the cameras of the time. Lee was asked to slow down so the blur of his fists could be captured on film, then the footage was slowed down further in the edit so the audience could perceive the punches. That's how fast he was! Lee went on to star in a few films showcasing his martial arts skills, including *The Way of the Dragon* (1972) and *Enter the Dragon* (1973).

The Coin Trickster

Lee's speed is legendary – even more so because he died at 32, before his acting career really had the chance to take off. One party trick he was known for was grabbing a coin out of someone's hand so fast they barely knew it had happened. Standing a few feet away, he'd tell an unsuspecting volunteer to close their fist around the coin in their palm as soon as they saw him move. They would, only to look down and see their coin replaced with another and a smug Lee, holding theirs, back in his starting spot.

Who built the Hollywood sign?

The Hollywood sign, recognised the world over, has become synonymous with Los Angeles's prolific film industry. But when it was originally constructed in 1923, it was as a rather expensive advertisement for a new property development called Hollywoodland. The original 14-metre-high sign included 'land' at the end and was illuminated by 4,000 lightbulbs.

THE BIRTH OF AN INDUSTRY

Hollywood was founded as a California district in 1887. The origins of the name are not certain, but it's thought that one of the district's founders met a woman on the train whose summer home had that name, or that it was a reference to the area's red-berried toyon shrub, also known as California holly. In 1910 – a year before the first film studio opened there – Hollywood merged with Los Angeles.

Scaling Up

Los Angeles Times publisher Harry Chandler's upscale property development advertisement cost him and his partners $21,000 (equivalent to £235,000 today). Tinseltown was booming, and he wanted in on the property gold mine. The flashing sign, which mules hauled up the side of the mountain, might have been a big gamble, but it paid off. When the development opened, Chandler's newspaper declared it the first hillside residential development in the United States, and ads warned people of the 'ever-present danger to the children of big cities' and urged them to 'Come to Hollywoodland'. Immediately, 120 buyers signed contracts – but the dream was not to be. When the Great Depression struck at the end of the 1920s, the partners' other investments took a hit, and construction on the development was abruptly halted.

A Nip and a Tuck

Like many of Hollywood's stars, the Hollywood sign has had a few facelifts over the years. Only ever intended to last for 18 months, the original sign was constructed from 1-metre by 3-metre metal squares, held together by scaffolding built from telephone poles, wires and pipes. As a result of the sign's temporary nature, it needed constant maintenance, which stopped around the time the Hollywoodland dream collapsed during the Depression; for a while, the sign read 'Ollywoodland', after the H toppled over. In 1949, the Hollywood Chamber of Commerce stepped in to restore the whole sign, with the exception of the last four letters.

Celebrity Saviours

Hollywood celebrities have taken it upon themselves to keep the sign in good condition. A 1978 alliance, which included Alice Cooper, Andy Williams and *Playboy* founder Hugh Hefner, saw the stars pledge $28,000 each to fund a replacement. There was a three-month period without a sign, while it was replaced with a more structurally sound version with steel footings. The land it stands on is now owned by the City of Los Angeles after it was purchased in 2010 by another alliance of famous faces and brands, including Tom Hanks, Norman Lear and the Walt Disney Company. For the pricey sum of $12.5 million (around £9.8 million), the land surrounding the sign is now safe from development – ironically, the very thing it was originally advertising.

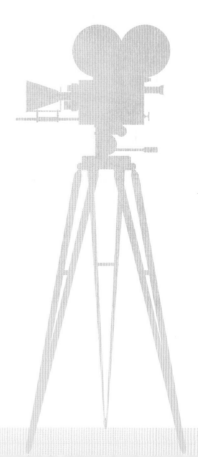

Does a show have to be on Broadway to be a Broadway show?

When people think of theatre, they think of 'Broadway'. The word conjures up images of chorus lines, glitzy theatres and extravagant performances. It's named for the New York City street central to the neighbourhood where the first grand theatres were opened in midtown Manhattan in the late 1800s and early 1900s.

Give My Regards to Broadway

For a show to be considered a 'Broadway show', it doesn't have to be running in a theatre situated on that street. Generally, the term refers to the 41 theatres in the district with over 499 seats. At the turn of the 20th century, when the term was first used to describe the scale of a show, a number of theatres were located on Broadway; today, only four 'Broadway' theatres actually have Broadway addresses, while many of the others are located on side streets that intersect with Broadway.

Off the Broadway Track

If a New York show is in a theatre with 99 to 499 seats, it's considered to be an Off-Broadway production. Most of these theatres are located in Greenwich Village and the Upper West Side. And if there are fewer than 99 seats, it's referred to as Off-Off-Broadway. These shows tend to be more experimental, while Broadway shows are largely big-budget musicals. Often a successful show that starts as Off-Broadway goes on to become a Broadway show after it's found an audience in a smaller theatre. A recent example is the phenomenal success of *Hamilton*, which had a six-month sold-out run Off-Broadway before moving to a Broadway theatre.

FILM AND THEATRE

QUIZ

There's no business like show business! And there's nothing people love more than an entertainment buff. Here's your chance to prove you're a star.

Questions

1. The dog playing Toto in *The Wizard of Oz* was paid more than Judy Garland – true or false?

2. Since 1652, who has performed traditional Japanese Kabuki?

3. During a production of which play did the original Globe theatre burn to the ground: *Henry VIII*, *Mamma Mia!* or *Cats*?

4. *The Phantom of the Opera* is set in the opera house of which European city?

5. What is Nigeria's film industry known as?

6. Complete the title of this famous Bruce Lee film: *Enter the____*.

7. The Hollywood sign was originally advertising a property development – true or false?

8. What was Thespis of Icaria the first person to do?

9. Are New York's 'Broadway' theatres all on the street Broadway?

10. *Hamlet* has been translated into *Star Trek*'s Klingon language – true or false?

Turn to page 249 for the answers.

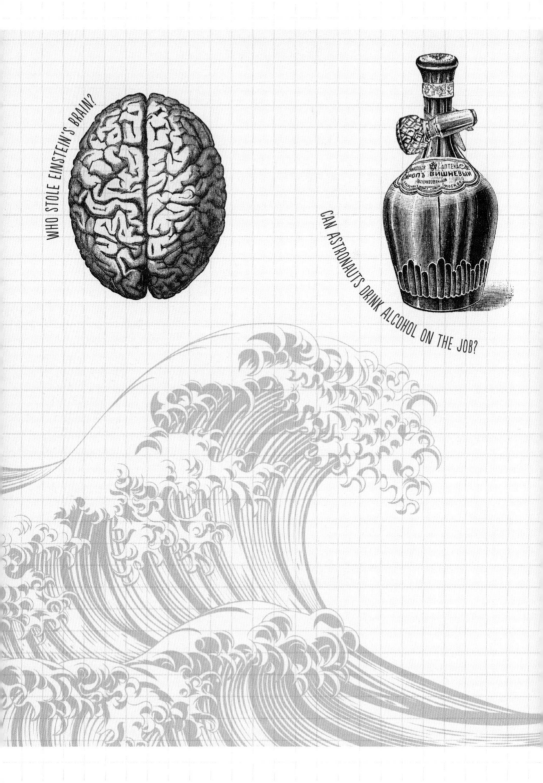

WHO STOLE EINSTEIN'S BRAIN?

CAN ASTRONAUTS DRINK ALCOHOL ON THE JOB?

Would life on Earth be better without the Moon?

The Moon is currently moving away from Earth at a rate of 3.78 centimetres every year as its orbit gets bigger. That's the same speed at which your fingernails grow. But if things sped up to the point that the Moon was no longer around, what would life on Earth be like?

Changing Tides

The Moon is kept in our orbit because of the gravitational force that Earth exerts on it, and the Moon exerts a gravitational force on Earth, which is responsible for our changing tides. There is more gravitational pull on the side of Earth that is facing the Moon than on the centre of the planet and the side facing away from it. This causes the oceans' water to stretch outwards on either side, which is known as 'tidal bulge'. As the Earth rotates throughout the day, the pull causes high tides twice a day, followed by low tides six hours later. Without the Moon there would still be tides, because the Sun has an effect too, but they would be less extreme. The tides are important – they help move heat from the equator to the poles, bringing cyclical warm and cool temperatures. Species rely on these temperatures for migration, and their predictability is useful to fishers, military vessels and even surfers.

Is It Bedtime Yet?

As Earth rotates, it drags the position of these tidal bulges ahead of where they otherwise would be, directly under the Moon. The counteracting effect of the Moon on these tidal bulges results in friction that slows down Earth's rotation and pushes the Moon farther away, increasing its orbit. When the Moon was first formed, days on Earth (the time it takes to complete a full rotation) were only five hours long, but it has gradually moved away from our planet, this braking effect has increased the day length to our current 24 hours. If this process were to speed up, with the Moon disappearing into the distance, our days would get longer and longer. However, if we'd never had the Moon to begin with, we'd barely have time to get up and get to work before it was bedtime again.

Wobbly Planet

One benefit of having the Moon around is that it prevents Earth from wobbling while it spins. The Moon acts as a stabiliser, keeping Earth angled on its axis at a tilt of 23 degrees. Because of this tilt, the northern hemisphere sees longer days and warmer weather during its summer, when it's tilted closer to the Sun. Without the Moon, Earth would be unstable and parts of the world would have to deal with more extreme temperature swings than we're currently used to.

DRIFTING APART

Scientific simulations imply that when the Moon was formed 4.5 billion years ago, it was positioned much closer to home – only 22,500 kilometres away. Today that distance is 402,336 kilometres. And in 265 years it will have advanced by another kilometre.

What happened to the Soviet space dogs?

Between 1951 and 1966, the Soviets pulled ahead in the Space Race after betting their money on dogs to pave the way for humans. While over a dozen dogs didn't survive to wag their tails another day, those that did became Soviet heroes for their service to space travel.

Why Dogs?

Before the days of manned space travel and the International Space Station, both American and Soviet space agencies relied on animals to test the limits of what was possible.

The Americans sent monkeys and chimpanzees up to the stars, but the Soviets decided dogs were calmer and would be better able to handle the stress than other animals. Monkeys, they thought, were more likely to succumb to disease. Rather than breed dogs specifically for the purpose, or source pedigree champions, they decided street mutts, adept at handling Moscow's extreme winters and accustomed to hunger, would be most capable of handling the pressures of space travel. Canine candidates had to be between 6 and 7 kilos, aged between one-and-a-half and six, female (because it would be easier for them to urinate in the small capsules), and with light-coloured fur so they would show up on cameras.

The First Dogs in Space

On 15 August 1951, two dogs, Dezik and Tsygan, became the first mammals to successfully survive a suborbital flight. They reached a height of 100 kilometres before their rocket's nose cone parachuted them safely back to Earth. Travelling at a speed of 4,180 kilometres per hour apparently had no lasting adverse effects on the dogs, which were wagging their tails when

Soviet Heroes

The first dog in orbit was Laika – she was sent up with the second Soviet satellite, *Sputnik II*, in 1957. While for years it was thought Laika survived up to seven days in space, in 2002 it was revealed that she had actually died within a few hours of the launch due to a thermal conductivity miscalculation. No recovery system was put in place for Laika's mission, meaning she was seen around the world as a victim of the Space Race.

Laika's achievements were soon eclipsed in 1960 by Belka and Strelka, the first animals to be recovered successfully from orbit. They were international celebrities, appearing on television, meeting important politicians, and becoming the faces of Soviet space travel. One of Strelka's puppies, Pushinka, was even given as a present to President John F. Kennedy's daughter, although not before the Secret Service had examined the pup for bugging devices.

they were released from the capsule. The two dogs were part of a nine-strong pack put through the training programme to prepare for the flight. Dezik was back up a week later with another dog called Lisa; unfortunately, the rocket's parachute failed to open and both dogs died. Launch security officer Anatoly Blagon didn't want Tsygan to face the same fate, so he adopted her and took her home to Moscow, where she lived a long life.

How big is the Milky Way?

Our solar system – made up of the Sun, eight planets, dwarf planets and natural satellites, such as our Moon – is located in an outer spiral arm of the Milky Way galaxy. Neptune, the farthest planet from our Sun, is located nearly 4.35 billion kilometres from Earth. And beyond *our* solar system is the rest of the galaxy.

Big Black Hole

There are four major arms to the Milky Way, and they're made up of at least 100 billion stars. The distance across the galaxy is about 100,000 light-years. It's hard to fathom how far that is, but one light-year is approximately 9 trillion kilometres. In the centre is a massive black hole, estimated to be about 4 million times bigger than our Sun. Our solar system, along with all the other stars, is orbiting around that black hole, travelling at speeds of 828,000 kilometres per hour. But it's so huge that it takes 230 million years to get all the way around.

Keep It Local

Parts of our galaxy are believed to be around 13.5 billion years old, which is only a few hundred million years younger than the universe itself. It is part of a collection of 30 galaxies known as the Local Group. The largest member is the Andromeda Galaxy, and the Milky Way is the second largest. The Local Group is just one of many galaxy clusters that are moving away from each other as the universe expands.

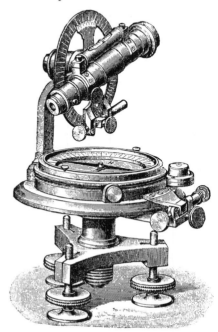

Why don't we feel the Earth moving?

Unless you live near the poles, where things turn slightly slower, you're currently sitting atop a giant rock spinning on its axis at a constant speed of 1,675 kilometres per hour (465 metres per second). But because planet Earth is so darn big, you don't feel a thing.

Head in the Clouds

Because Earth's atmosphere is moving at the same speed you are, you don't feel the speed the planet is travelling at. Being on Earth is a bit like travelling on a plane, but twice as fast. Because a plane is travelling so quickly, when it's not speeding up or slowing down you can close your eyes and barely perceive the fact you're moving at 800 kilometres per hour. The only way you can really tell is by looking outside and seeing the clouds.

Prepare for Landing

Beyond Earth's rotating atmosphere are the Moon, Sun and stars, which all give us an indication that we're moving. But because we're so far from them, and the change is slow, constant and gradual, it almost looks like they're moving and we're constant, which is what our ancestors thought. If Earth

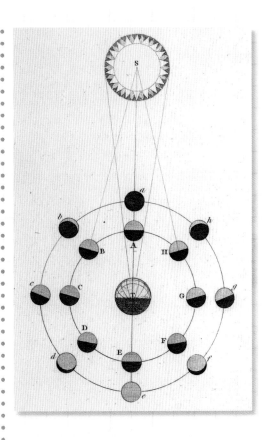

were to suddenly speed up or slow down, like a plane coming in to land, you'd be sure to feel it. It's unlikely, though. For our planet to stop rotating or to rotate at a different speed, it would have to be unbalanced by an unimaginable external force – a collision on an interplanetary scale.

What are the chances of getting hit by a meteor?

A meteor is the spectacular streak of light you see trailing behind a meteoroid as it enters Earth's atmosphere. If a meteoroid crash-lands on Earth, it becomes a meteorite. Thus, the chances of getting hit by a meteor are none, but there's a minuscule chance that a meteorite could get you.

Slim Chance

A meteoroid is a small interplanetary object that's orbiting the Sun; they're often particles that have broken off from asteroids or comets. Each day, about four billion meteoroids fall to Earth, but most of them are tiny in size – no bigger than a speck of dust – and vaporise as they enter Earth's atmosphere. It's rare that anything much bigger manages to get through. According to NASA, about once a year a car-sized asteroid hits Earth's atmosphere, but most of it burns up on entry. Some do make it through, however; a 1985 study calculated that the rate at which humans are hit by meteorites is 0.0055 per year, or one event in every 180 years.

Bruised by a Meteorite

This particularly rare honour, if you can call it that, was bestowed upon Ann Hodges in 1954. While she napped on her couch in Sylacauga, Alabama, United States, a 4.7-kilo meteorite about the size of an orange crashed through the ceiling, bounced off a radio and hit her on the hip. Other than the shock and a large football-shaped bruise, she was unharmed. After the US Air Force confirmed the black object was in fact a meteorite, a legal battle ensued between Ann Hodges and her

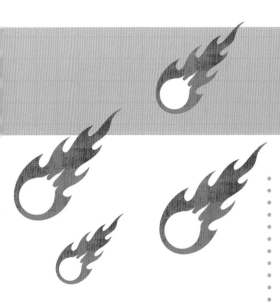

landlady regarding to whom it belonged. Ann's landlady felt that she had ownership of the rock, given that it fell on her property, but eventually settled out of court for $500. Ann and her husband hoped to sell the meteorite for a small fortune, but after big offers were not forthcoming, they donated it to the Alabama Museum of Natural History, where it still resides.

HOT ROCKS

Approximately 24,000 meteorites have been found on Earth, but there are many that have yet to be found in the oceans or remote, uninhabited locations. The latest research suggests between 100 and 2,000 meteorites land on Earth each year. If you're lucky enough to find one, you might be able to make a few quid. Space rocks tend to go for around £1.50 per gram – they're worth even more if someone saw them fall. The Holy Grail is a bit of the Moon or Mars, which can fetch up to £780 per gram. But you might need to pack your bags and head to Antarctica or North Africa to find them, because these reddish rocks are much easier to spot on ice or sand dunes.

Who stole Einstein's brain?

After eminent physicist Albert Einstein died of a ruptured aneurysm in the early hours of 18 April 1955, his body wound up in the morgue at Princeton Hospital in New Jersey, Unites States. Presiding over the autopsy was the on-call pathologist, Thomas Stoltz Harvey, who would become known as the man who stole Einstein's brain.

Was It Really Theft?

The jury will probably always be out over whether Einstein wanted his brain to be studied. Some have reported that he left strict instructions for his remains to be cremated and his ashes scattered in secret, to avoid a grave site becoming a shrine to him and his work. But others, notably Ronald Clark in his 1984 biography, have written that Einstein insisted his brain should be used for research.

Rather than simply identifying and confirming the cause of death, Harvey sawed open Einstein's skull and removed his brain. He also removed his eyes and gave them to the physicist's eye doctor. The family's permission was not sought until after Harvey had taken ownership of the organ; Einstein's son, Hans Albert, was furious when he learned that his father's dying wishes had not been met, but was convinced by Harvey to grant permission, in the hope his father's brain would reveal the very nature of genius.

Preserving Genius

After the autopsy, Harvey weighed and measured this 'genius' brain. It weighed 1.2 kilos, towards the lower end of the normal range for a man of 76. He then took the brain to a laboratory at the University of Pennsylvania, United States, where a rare instrument, called a microtone, was used to divide the brain into microscopic sections, which were embedded in celloidin – a chemical that hardens tissue. There were believed to be 240 pieces in total. Many of these slides were sent to the leading neuropathologists of the day, but none of them found anything notable about the brain, and their findings were never published.

Returning the Relic

After effectively stealing Einstein's brain, Harvey's career never recovered. He lost his job at Princeton Hospital and then lost his medical license in the late 1980s for failing a competency examination. He ended up working on the assembly line at a plastic extrusion factory, and died in 2007. A 1978 interview with Harvey renewed interest in the scientist's brain, and a number of studies were conducted, with inconclusive results. In 1998, Harvey handed over the remaining 170 pieces of Einstein's brain in his possession to the chief pathologist at the University Medical Center of Princeton – the contemporary name for Princeton Hospital.

PRECIOUS EYES

Einstein's eyes are believed to be peering into the darkness of a New Jersey safe-deposit box. Einstein's ophthalmologist, Henry Abrams, remained the owner of the eyes for the rest of his life – he died in 2009, aged 97. In a 1994 interview, he denied the eyes would go up for auction, saying: 'Having his eyes means the professor's life has not ended. A part of him is still with me.' They've still not been sold publicly.

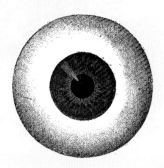

What's on the far side of the Moon?

When the Soviet *Luna 3* spacecraft captured the far side of the Moon on camera for the first time in 1959, the result was shocking. There might not have been little green men hiding out there, but the landscape was markedly different from the side we'd all been staring at for millennia.

Far, Far Away

The Moon is tidally locked in place, meaning the same side always faces Earth. The first humans to see the surface with their own eyes were the crew of *Apollo 8*, who orbited the Moon in 1968. While the near side has huge regions of ancient lava flows, called maria, caused by volcanic activity, the far side is littered with crater impacts; the crust is thicker, making it more difficult for magmas to erupt on the surface, creating a completely different appearance.

Beware of the Dark Side

Many people mistake the 'far side' of the Moon for the 'dark side', probably because of Pink Floyd's hugely successful 1973 album entitled *The Dark Side of the Moon*. There is a dark side of the Moon, as the Moon, like Earth, has daytime and night-time. However, as on Earth, that 'side' is constantly changing. If you were able to set up camp on the far side of the Moon, you'd experience both day and night. But because it takes the Moon around 29 Earth days to complete one full rotation on its axis around the Sun, as well as a complete orbit around Earth, you would experience two weeks of daytime, then two weeks of night-time.

Does space need cleaning?

Space is a very messy place. There are over 500,000 pieces of debris orbiting Earth at any given time, some 20,000 times larger than an orange. This space junk can travel at speeds up to 30,000 kilometres per hour, and even a tiny piece can cause major damage to a satellite or spacecraft.

Man-made Mess

There are two types of space debris: natural meteoroids, orbiting the Sun, and particles from man-made objects, orbiting Earth and known as 'orbital debris'. The latter is made up of larger items like non-functional spacecraft and abandoned launch vehicle components. With over 1,071 operational satellites orbiting Earth, it's important that this debris is monitored and that future waste is minimised as much as possible.

Cleaning It Up

In 1995, NASA issued a set of guidelines for the mitigation of orbital debris. As well as preventing the creation of new debris, their measures involve designing satellites that can withstand the impact of small debris, and manoeuvering spacecraft and satellites where necessary to avoid major collisions. Another tactic is controlled re-entry, where a more accurate landing position can be calculated over an uninhabited area, such as the ocean, for any bits of debris that don't decay on re-entry. The year 2017 also sees the launch of RemoveDEBRIS, a multimillion-dollar mission funded by the European Commission and led by the Surrey Space Centre in the UK, to test a range of space-cleaning devices. In the first mission of its kind, a platform of harpoon, net and sail devices will be launched into space and tested using artificial junk.

Why haven't we met any aliens?

Maybe we've just not been looking hard enough. Our Sun is one of up to 400 billion stars in The Milky Way, one of the universe's 100 billion galaxies. If all those stars have on average one planet orbiting them, that's an awful lot of space for us mere mortals to scope out.

The Great Silence

A 2013 study used data from the Kepler space telescope to assert that one in five Sun-like stars has an Earth-sized planet orbiting in the habitable region, where liquid water is possible, allowing life to flourish. The fact that we've yet to find evidence of extraterrestrial civilisation in our galaxy or beyond, given how likely it is that it exists, poses the question: Why haven't aliens visited our planet yet? This has become known as the Fermi paradox: 'the great silence'.

WHOSE PARADOX?

Enrico Fermi raised the idea of the great silence in 1950, and it has troubled scientists ever since. Fermi won the Nobel Prize in Physics for his work into radioactivity. He'd left Italy for a new life in America and went on to build a prototype for a nuclear reactor. He also worked on the Manhattan Project to develop the first atomic bomb.

Filtered Out

One possible explanation for the Fermi paradox is the 'great filter' hypothesis. This suggests that an obstacle stands in the way of ordinary dead matter becoming 'advanced exploding lasting life' and prevents other life forms from developing enough to reach us. The theory also suggests that the 'great filter' could still be ahead of planet Earth, and without proof that we've already overcome it – such as through the emergence of reproductive molecules or simple single-celled life in our planet's ancient history – we must assume that some great catastrophe lies in wait for us.

Too Far Apart

Another suggestion is that while there might be other intelligent life out there, we're just too far apart to communicate. However, another life form might pick up on a message we've sent, even if they can't reply. With this in mind, in 1974 a transmission known as the 'Arecibo message' was sent using a radio telescope to the Hercules Globular Cluster of about 300,000 stars. It contained 1,679 binary digits that communicated, among other things,

the numbers one to ten, the population of Earth and a graphic of the double helix structure of DNA. The message was sent only once – symbolically, to show it could be done – and we've yet to hear anything back.

Breakthrough the Silence

Our extraterrestrial treasure hunt has so far been fairly limited – the Hubble Telescope has performed only one atmospheric study of an Earth-sized planet. But in 2015 a £78 million project called Breakthrough Listen launched a plan to change that by carrying out a survey of the closest million stars, our galaxy and the 100 nearest galaxies. This comprehensive study, expected to take ten years, hopes to find a definitive answer to the Fermi paradox, using powerful radio telescopes for signals.

Do astronauts eat their veggies?

In 1961, Soviet cosmonaut Gherman Titov became the first human to consume food in space, followed in 1962 by the first American, John Glenn. Titov tucked into soup, liver food paste, and blackcurrant juice, while Glenn ate apple sauce through a squeezy tube. But today's astronauts do a little better than that.

Cosmic Dining

With over half a century of space exploration and scientific development, eating in space has improved significantly since the 1960s. Astronauts make their menu choices preflight from a wide variety of options, many containing fruits and vegetables. However, most meals consist of rehydratable food and/or thermostabilised food, heat-treated to destroy any potentially harmful microorganisms. Rehydratable food is ideal for space travel as it's lighter, takes up less space and the water needed to prepare it is available in abundance – it's a by-product of the space shuttle fuel cells.

The first apples, bananas, and carrot and celery sticks were flown on the space shuttle in 1983, and since then fresh fruit and vegetables are always included. Fresh produce is also taken to the International Space Station (ISS) via resupply cargo vehicles, but must be consumed within a few days due to the lack of refrigeration on board.

Veg-01

In 2015, Exhibition 44 crew members on board the ISS ate the first space-grown food as part of an experiment known as Veg-01. Nicknamed 'Veggie' by NASA, the result of years of work was a red romaine lettuce, and according to astronaut Scott Kelly, it tasted 'good. Kinda like arugula [rocket]'.

The Veggie system, about the size of a stovetop, uses red and blue LEDs – which emit the most light – to stimulate plant growth. But for the lettuce, green LEDs were added, to make the plant more recognisable and therefore more appetising. The seeds are activated in rooting 'pillows' – chambers consisting of clay, fertiliser, and water – and the lettuce was ready for harvest after about a month. It wasn't the first lettuce grown in space; its predecessor was also a horticultural success, but was flown back to Earth for testing, rather than risk any contamination by the astronauts.

In 2016, the first flower to be grown successfully in space – a zinnia, part of the daisy family – bloomed for the first time on the ISS. The next space gardening experiment, due to start in 2018, plans to grow tomatoes in low Earth orbit.

THE BENEFITS OF SPACE GARDENING

The ISS has nowhere near enough space to facilitate a large-scale garden, but the experiments taking place there are the first steps towards making space missions more sustainable. Space flights are restricted by the amount of supplies that can be carried onboard, or must rely on being resupplied. But if astronauts were able to grow some of their own food, they could travel for longer, exploring deeper into space. It's also believed that growing fresh food has a positive impact on the astronauts' state of mind, providing a welcome hobby and helping with stress for those on longer space missions.

Who's spent the most time in space?

Russian Gennady Ivanovich Padalka holds the world record for the most time spent in space by a human – 879 days, spanning five missions. Before taking off for the fifth in March 2015, during which he celebrated his 57th birthday, he declared his aim of spending 1,000 days in space during his career.

Russian Veterans

Padalka was selected for cosmonaut training in 1989, having risen to the rank of colonel in the Soviet air force. His first mission was in 1998, when he

became one of the last cosmonauts to spend time on the *Mir* space station, preparing it for deactivation and de-orbit. He has now enjoyed four visits to the International Space Station (ISS), spending two of those tours as station commander, and carrying out nine space walks. He was commanding the ISS in 2009 when the space shuttle *Endeavour* docked and unloaded its crew. The seven newcomers boosted the total number onboard to 13 – the largest ever human gathering in space in one craft.

Fellow Russian Valeri Polyakov holds the record for longest individual space flight, spending 438 days aboard the *Mir* space station between 1994 and 1995. Extended space trips are extremely hard on the body. Because there's no gravity, the muscles we use against Earth's gravitational force have little work to do, resulting in muscle atrophy. Astronauts also face a decrease in bone density, because bone tissue breaks down faster than it builds up. There are also the extreme psychological challenges faced by those spending months – 14, in Polyakov's case – in the confines of a space station.

The New Space Race

The Americans have a long way to go to match Padalka's record. In 2016, Jeffrey Williams broke the American record by spending 534 days in space across four missions – likely to be exceeded by fellow American Peggy Whitson, who will bring her total up to 560 days after completing her 2016–17 mission. Whitson was also the first woman to command the ISS, and the oldest woman to blast off into space when she set out on this latest mission. NASA's astronauts hold other records, too. James Voss and Susan Helms hold the joint record for the longest space walks, spending eight hours and 56 minutes outside the space shuttle *Discovery* and the ISS in 2001, while Franklin Chang-Diaz and Jerry Ross share the record for most trips to space, both having made seven space flights throughout their careers. And to top that off, as of 2016, the ISS has had 226 different visitors from 18 different countries. More have been American (142) than any other nationality.

'Astronauts face a decrease in bone density, because bone tissue breaks down faster than it builds up.'

LIVE THE DREAM

If you have the cash to spare, you too could make space history by buying a stay in space. At a cost of somewhere around the £27 million mark, you could buy a ticket to the space station. Someone who knows the thrill of this extravagant holiday is Charles Simonyi. The American software billionaire has taken two two-week trips to space at a cost of £19.5 million and £27 million respectively.

Can astronauts drink alcohol on the job?

For most of us, the thought of spending weeks trapped in a confined capsule in space is enough to drive us to drink, but the truth is, while alcohol is sent on space missions for experimental purposes, astronauts aren't allowed to drink it. Although that hasn't always been the case...

Sherry Bad Idea

When NASA launched *Skylab*, the world's first space station, in 1973, it almost became the first bar in space, too. Original menu planning for the astronauts included sherry, deemed to be the most stable type of wine because it is heated during processing. Paul Masson California Rare Cream Sherry was selected from taste tests and ordered for the mission. A flexible plastic pouch package with a built-in drinking tube was developed to house the booze. But it seemed public opinion was opposed to any wild space

parties and NASA's alcohol programme came to an abrupt end. *Skylab*'s manager listed a number of reasons for the change of heart, including the expectation of 'continued criticism and ridicule ... if such a beverage is provided.'

Russian Rebels

The strict NASA rules mean that American astronauts have no place for alcohol on the International Space Station, whereas Russian cosmonauts have had a much more relaxed approach to booze on board. Since the earliest Russian space flights, and particularly on the *Mir* space station, alcohol was a key part of the crew's rations. Former *Mir* crew member Alexander Lazutkin said that cognac was recommended by doctors 'to stimulate the cosmonauts' immune system'.

SPACE TRAVEL AND THE UNIVERSE

If this section helped you expand your mind, now's the time to test what you've learned. And if you get stuck, don't panic. The truth is out there!

Questions

1. When the Moon was formed, was it closer to Earth or farther away from Earth than it is now?

2. Which American president's daughter received a puppy that was the offspring of one of the space dogs in the Russian space programme?

3. Earth is spinning at 322 kilometres per hour – true or false?

4. Did Einstein's brain weigh considerably more than the average male's?

5. Was it a Soviet or a US spacecraft that first photographed the far side of the Moon?

6. There are over 500,000 pieces of debris in space orbiting Earth – true or false?

7. What alcoholic drink almost became part of the *Skylab* menu?

8. What was the Arecibo message: a message from aliens, a message to aliens or a message to humans in space?

9. What was the first vegetable to be grown and eaten in space?

10. Record-holder Valeri Polyakov spent four continuous years in space – true or false?

Turn to page 249 for the answers.

QUIZ ANSWERS

Weather and Climate Quiz Answers

1. False. They will always be different on a molecular level, despite looking the same.
2. The longer it takes the snowman to burn, the longer winter will be.
3. Algae. It's edible – but you might want to avoid eating it due to its laxative effect!
4. Fog.
5. Nor'easter, *purga*, *metel'*, *v'yuga*, *buran*.
6. True.
7. Slower.
8. Fish, frogs, snails, toads, tadpoles, alligator.
9. False. He was trying to prove it was a form of electricity.
10. Hurricanes.

The Human Body Quiz Answers

1. A 60-year-old.
2. Rabies.
3. Tickly cough, dementia, cancer, diabetes.
4. Their own way of talking.
5. Urine.
6. True.
7. False. Green is the rarest.
8. More – as much as 7% in some cases.
9. Red and white (and sometimes blue, too).
10. An Indian healer known as Sushruta recorded the first cosmetic surgeries at some point between 1000 and 600 BCE.

Art and Architecture Quiz Answers

1. False. It was for his third wife, Mumtaz Mahal.
2. The Eiffel Tower.
3. The seven continents.
4. True.
5. His right ear.
6. It's too far away. The Moon is 384,400 kilometres from our planet.
7. Four: two pastels and two paintings.
8. Campbell's.
9. False. It's based on David from the biblical story of David and Goliath.
10. Mexico.

Animals and Plants Quiz Answers

1. Giraffe.
2. Its painful sting.
3. False. It's found in a dog's nose and is also known as the vomeronasal organ.
4. The blue whale.
5. Parrot.
6. True.
7. Large. The size of their brain in relation to their body is second only to humans.
8. Their diet of algae and shrimp.
9. East, because they react more strongly to the early morning light.
10. True.

Ancient History Quiz Answers

1. Kayaking.
2. False. There was a white granite quarry at the top of the mountain.
3. To build up immunity to poisons, due to the threat of assassination.
4. A famous document. Magna Carta established important principles in English law in the 13th century.
5. Water shows where epic battle re-enactments took place.
6. Their heads and their teeth.
7. The tomb of China's first emperor, Qin Shi Huang, in Shaanxi Province.
8. False. They were entitled to one-third of it.
9. The Aztecs (or Mexica).
10. Being soldiers.

Food and Drink Quiz Answers

1. More at risk.
2. Tea – 2.35 trillion cups are produced every year, compared to 850 billion cups of coffee.
3. Queen Victoria.
4. False. A *salarium* was a soldier's salary.
5. Chiclets chewing gum.
6. United States.
7. Chillies.
8. Dr Pepper.
9. Gin.
10. The pig.

Literature Quiz Answers

1. It allowed an author to sign books from thousands of kilometres away. Margaret Atwood was the first to use it.
2. Cadbury.
3. The Harry Potter books by J. K. Rowling.
4. Mark Twain.
5. Klingon.
6. Spy for the US government.
7. Butterflies.
8. Voice.
9. It was shredded by his dog.
10. False. He was named after a black bear named 'Winnie' and a toy swan named 'Pooh'.

Geography Quiz Answers

1. Antarctica.
2. True.
3. Peru.
4. James Cameron.
5. The Amazon.
6. Mount Everest.
7. Arizona.
8. Las Vegas.
9. The Bermuda Triangle.
10. True.

Sports Quiz Answers

1. True.
2. Waffles.
3. The bullseye.
4. Tidal bores.
5. Golf.
6. Jumping with a parachute from a low altitude, such as off a building or cliff.
7. False. They were introduced after research showed they were more visible to television audiences.
8. American football.
9. To dig his own starting blocks.
10. False. They wear a yellow jersey. The polka-dot jersey is worn by the rider with the best climber ranking.

Science Quiz Answers

1. Brown.
2. Sun protection factor.
3. Slows down.
4. Plastic.
5. False. There is no evidence to suggest this. However, it's believed yawning helps cool down the brain.
6. Dark chocolate, because of the higher concentrations of theobromine.
7. The Third Reich, run by the Nazis.
8. No. Four elements were added in 2015, with more yet to be discovered.
9. Red.
10. False. Luminol can help show where blood, bleach and even horseradish have been, but not ketchup.

Film and Theatre Quiz Answers

1. False. But he was paid more than the actors playing the Munchkins.
2. Teenage boys.
3. *Henry VIII.*
4. Paris.
5. Nollywood.
6. *Dragon.*
7. True.
8. Act.
9. No. Only four of the 41 Broadway theatres are on Broadway.
10. True.

Space Travel and the Universe Quiz Answers

1. It was closer to Earth.
2. John F. Kennedy's daughter.
3. False. It's actually spinning at 1,675 kilometres per hour.
4. No. In fact, it weighed towards the lower end of the normal range for a man of his age.
5. A Soviet spacecraft: *Luna 3.*
6. True.
7. Sherry.
8. A message to aliens. It was a 1974 transmission sent to 300,000 stars in the hope of contacting other intelligent life forms.
9. Romaine lettuce.
10. False. But he has spent 438 consecutive days there.

INDEX

CREDITS

1, 3, 185 © lynea | Shutterstock • 6, 31, 76 © ilbusca | iStock, Voropaev Vasiliy | Shutterstock, gjebic nicolae | Shutterstock • 8, 236 © Dimonika | Shutterstock • 9, 31, 39, 42, 73, 193, 228 © Hein Nouwens | Shutterstock • 14 © anussa | Shutterstock • 17 © Chronicle | Alamy Stock Photo• 18, 48, 49 © Wellcome Images• 20, 101 © vectorEps | Shutterstock • 21 © Eric Isselee | Shutterstock • 23 © Melok | Shutterstock • 24 © notbad | Shutterstock • 28 © logaryphmic | Shutterstock • 30 © Kamira | Shutterstock • 30, 91 © Betacam-SP | Shutterstock • 30, 38 © Prokhorovich | Shutterstock • 34 © AF archive | Alamy Stock Photo • 35 © Nicku | Shutterstock • 36 © H. ARMSTRONG ROBERTS | Alamy Stock Photo • 40 © adehoidar | Shutterstock • 41 © Melica | Shutterstock • 43 © Courtesy Everett Collection | Alamy Stock Photo • 44, 46, 50, 59, 94, 98, 109, 128, 188, 209, 233 © Morphart Creation | Shutterstock • 47, 88 © Creative Commons • 47 © Tony Baggett | Shutterstock • 49 © Rosa Jay | Shutterstock • 52, 66, 138, 178, 208 © Everett Historical | Shutterstock • 57 © The Protected Art Archive | Alamy Stock Photo, Vector Tradition SM | Shutterstock, charl898 | Shutterstock • 58 © best4u | Shutterstock • 61 © Luciano Mortula - LGM | Shutterstock • 62 © Art Reserve | Alamy Stock Photo • 63 © muratart | Shutterstock • 65 © Baurz1973 | Shutterstock • 68 © Andrew Unangst | Alamy Stock Photo • 72 © Patrick K. Campbell | Shutterstock • 75, 120, 200, 255 © INTERFOTO | Alamy Stock Photo • 78 © Emilio Ereza | Alamy Stock Photo • 80 © Krylovochka | Shutterstock • 81 © Stocksnapper | Shutterstock, Real PIX | Shutterstock • 82 © GrayGooseGosling | iStock • 83 © ArchMan | Shutterstock. Robert Adrian Hillman | Shutterstock • 84–85 © cynoclub | iStock • 89 © Brandon Blinkenberg | Shutterstock • 91 © Coprid | Shutterstock • 92 © oksana2010 | Shutterstock • 96 © flocu | Shutterstock • 97 © Ian Dyball | Shutterstock • 99, 141 © Granger Historical Picture Archive | Alamy Stock Photo • 103 © testing | Shutterstock • 106 © Alis Leonte | Shutterstock • 108 © Anastasios71 | Shutterstock • 110 © Jjustas | Shutterstock, Sofiaworld | Shutterstock • 114 © ppi09 | Shutterstock • 115 © JGA | Shutterstock, Quang Ho | Shutterstock • 117 © GeorgePeters | iStock • 118 © Shaliapina | Shutterstock • 122 © whitemay | iStock • 123 © ILYA AKINSHIN | Shutterstock • 124 © andrey oleynik | Shutterstock • 128 © Sabelskaya | Shutterstock • 130, 142 © DoubleBubble | Shutterstock • 132 © Alex_Bond | Shutterstock • 133 © Drozzhina Elena | Shutterstock • 134 © newelle | Shutterstock • 135 © Sergey Roshchin | Shutterstock • 136 © Schwabenblitz | Shutterstock • 137 © Vladyslav Starozhylov | Shutterstock • 143 © EngravingFactory | Shutterstock • 144 © Yoko Design | Shutterstock, Glen Jones | Shutterstock • 146 © Everett Collection Historical | Alamy Stock Photo • 147 © benoitb | iStock • 148 © Dita | Shutterstock • 152 © VladimirCeresnak | Shutterstock • 153 © Rainer Lesniewski | Shutterstock • 154 © vectortatu | Shutterstock • 156, 161 © skelos | Shutterstock • 157 © Top Vector Studio | Shutterstock • 159 © Patryk Kosmider | Shutterstock • 162 © MSSA | Shutterstock • 164 © Chad Zuber | Shutterstock • 169 © Keystone Pictures USA | Alamy Stock Photo, okart | Shutterstock • 170 © Nataleana | Shutterstock, LANTERIA | Shutterstock • 171 © abrakadabra | Shutterstock, Firuz Salamzadeh | Shutterstock • 173 © gomolach | Shutterstock • 175 © RetroClipArt | Shutterstock • 176 © Aaron Amat | Shutterstock, Kluva | Shutterstock, Great_Kit | Shutetrstock • 177 © R3BV | Shutterstock • 179 © Brocreative | Shutterstock • 180 © pandora64 | Shutterstock • 182 © kstudija | Shutterstock • 186 © JONGSUK | Shutterstock • 188 © Yuliyan Velchev | Shutterstock • 194 © charobnica | Shutterstock • 196 © an_Half-tube | iStock • 199 © ALEXSTAND | Shutterstock • 202 © tan_tan | Shutterstock • 210 © BernardAllum | Shutterstock • 211 © mariia kalinina | Shutterstock • 212 © Everett Collection | Shutterstock • 214 © andersphoto | Shutterstock • 218 © Marzolino | Shutterstock • 224 © AstroStar | Shutterstock • 225 © Danussa | Shutterstock • 226 © Tairy Greene | Shutterstock • 227 © Heritage Image Partnership Ltd | Alamy Stock Photo • 229 © mashuk | iStock • 231 © Pavel Chagochkin | Shutterstock • 234 © FreshStream | iStock • 239 © gjebic nicolae | Shutterstock • 240 © CSA-Archive | Shutterstock • 251 © Leremy | Shutterstock • 252 © Vector FX | Shutterstock •